Winter
Herbal
Pleasures

Winter Herbal Pleasures

Preserving & Cooking With Herbs

Noël Richardson

Sterling Publishing Co., Inc.   New York

Library of Congress Cataloging-in-Publication Data

Richardson, Noël, 1937-
  Winter herbal pleasures : preserving and cooking with herbs / Noël
Richardson
      p.   cm.
  Originally published : Winter pleasures. Canada : Whitecap Books,
1990
  Includes bibliographical references and index.
  ISBN 0-8069-8348-5
  1. Cookery (Herbs)   2. Canning and preserving.   I. Title.
TX819.H4R55   1991
641.6'57—dc20   91-19413
                                           CIP

10 9 8 7 6 5 4 3 2 1

Published in 1991 by Sterling Publishing Company, Inc.
387 Park Avenue South, New York, N.Y. 10016

Originally published in Canada by Whitecap Books
as **Winter Pleasures** © 1990 by Noël Richardson

Line Drawings by Andrew Yeoman
Printed in Canada

Sterling ISBN 0-8069-8348-5

Contents

To Andrew Yeoman,
who grows the herbs,
chops the garlic and shallots,
eats my experiments and washes the pots!
Much love and thanks
for your support.

Introduction

*E*leven years ago, on July 1, 1979, Andrew Yeoman and I arrived at Ravenhill Farm (as yet unnamed). We had two tarragon plants, my fourteen-year-old daughter and a large French poodle. I was blissful to be returning to the island of my birth and we were full of dreams and plans about starting a herb farm. We planted our two tarragons and began our herbal journey. The first summer we collected herb plants and Andrew observed, sketched and planned our future garden. The second summer we sent out five letters to restaurants that we thought might be interested in buying fresh herbs. We received one telephone call, but by the end of the summer we had four customers. Our customers increased slowly — which was a good thing, as we were learning the business at the same time.

The next year, we produced a tiny cookbook with sixty recipes to encourage fresh herb use. I wrote the recipes and Andrew copied them out with his calligraphy pen. We printed it on a large copying machine and sold two thousand copies. A publisher became interested and I wrote *Summer Herbal Delights*, with illustrations by J. Ward-Harris. We began selling plants on Sundays in the spring and summer and people seemed to enjoy wandering through the garden, watching it grow and change. A few magazines wrote articles about the farm. People seemed intrigued that a former geologist-schoolteacher-investment consultant and a school librarian should end up happily growing herbs.

Book promotion led to cooking classes; now I do them in the newly renovated farm kitchen. The point of the classes is herbal and herbs are slipped into everything but coffee.

In the last decade there has been a herbal renaissance, as more people have rediscovered the many-faceted pleasures of growing, cooking and decorating with herbs. Herbs have so much to offer in the areas of taste, health, landscape and decoration, and they link us with a long, female domestic past that stretches back for centuries and is largely unrecorded. This may be one reason why women, in particular, have such a strong emotional response and attraction to herbs and herb gardens. They symbolize pleasure, comfort and beauty — vital qualities in a world that is often turbulent.

At Ravenhill we are completely absorbed in herbs. We read extensively in herb literature, focusing on culinary herbs and the cuisines that use them the most. We travel to France, Italy and California for culinary and herbal inspiration, and to England for landscaping and herb garden ideas. We have grown to love food that is fresh, simple, robust in flavor and laced with herbs. Everywhere we go, we search out the markets.

We return from our travels with many seed packets from France, Italy and California and, luckily for my cooking and writing, Andrew grows an amazing variety of herbs, greens and vegetables, with which I experiment and explore herbal cooking.

A year or so after *Summer Herbal Delights* was published, friends and booksellers started to ask the usual questions authors are asked. When is the next book? Will it be *Winter Herbal Pleasures*? A seed was sown, and I realized there was some form of herbal delights in our lives all year round. The mild, maritime climate of the Pacific coast enables the cook and gardener to have fresh herbs all winter. Not all herbs are pickable all winter, but most winters, barring an unseasonable cold snap which sets our rosemarys shivering and dying, I can pick and cook with a varied selection. Just before Christmas this year I picked bay leaves, rosemary, thyme, sage, Italian parsley, sorrel and winter savory. All of these herbs flavored our Christmas dinner beautifully and the final visual delight was surrounding the turkey with silver and red sage leaves and scattering rosemary and thyme sprigs across the large golden turkey breast.

Besides our hardy friends just mentioned, who do not take a winter rest as chives and tarragon do, there are all the herbs that can be preserved in various ways during the summer. Tucked away in cupboards or in your freezer, these herbs will spark up your winter cooking. Chives can be chopped and frozen in plastic bags. Tarragon can be preserved in vinegar, puréed in oil, or chopped and frozen. Sorrel can be puréed and frozen, basil can be stored in oil or frozen. These are just a few ways to capture summer herbs for winter.

Potting up herbs to have indoors is another way to have flavor in winter cooking, and some herbs take well to houseplant life. On my kitchen window still there is a small forest of plants that bring comfort all winter. There are two bay trees, two rosemary plants, and some basil. Winter savory, lemon thyme, thyme and sage will also grow well inside, as they do not need a dormant period. Lemon verbena will grow in the house, but will often drop its leaves in midwinter. I wait until spring for the other herbs. Seasonal surprises are actually a pleasure to the cook and gardener, not a deprivation.

In winter I focus on the pleasures of those herbs that are available. I have discovered some unique uses for rosemary, for example, either clipped from a potted plant or dried. I put it in French bread, on pizza, in biscuits, cocktail shortbread, and even in a hair rinse with vinegar and water. As generations of our female ancestors have learned, necessity and a narrowed selection can be a spur to creativity.

My cooking changes in winter. I bake more bread, make robust soups out of root vegetables, and flavor the rich stews in my clay cooker with the strong winter herbs: rosemary, savory, thyme and bay. The cooler weather affects the appetite, and the thought of a herby stew simmering while we are out hiking on a Sunday afternoon is truly a winter pleasure. I depend on those great winter flavor staples — garlic, shallots and onions — and as I chop them I think of the sunny days of summer when they were harvested and lay golden and rosy, spread out to cure in the sun.

I tend to use more spices in winter, such as cloves, cinnamon, mace and nutmeg. In *Winter Herbal Pleasures* I have included recipes using spices as well as herbs, as they are an integral part of winter cooking and Christmas celebrating.

Most of my recipes are short in length and long on flavor, emphasizing fresh ingredients perked up with herbal preserves. I have found that using herbs reduces or eliminates the need for salt in most recipes and many of these recipes call for no salt. You can use fresh or frozen herbs in all the recipes and occasionally dry may be substituted.

As one cook wryly said, cooking and eating are some of life's reliable pleasures. I hope my book brings much pleasure to the cooks who read it and use it.

Ravenhill Herb Farm, September 1990

CHAPTER ONE

Preserving Summer Delights for Winter Pleasures

The hard truth for the cook and herb gardener is summer does not last. There will not be endless basil and tomatoes in the garden. Herbs and vegetables will slowly wind down and one could end up in December like the proverbial grasshopper, with an empty cupboard. This chapter will provide many ideas for stocking that cupboard. Yes, you can have pesto in December!

I recommend you set aside a basket or shelf in your freezer for your preserved herbs. Label them well — we all have had the experience of finding mystery packages in our freezer that need carbon dating before they can be used. A cool dark cupboard for vinegars and jellies and dried herbs is also very useful. Many of the preserved herbs will make perfect hostess or Christmas gifts, and it is comforting to have such a stash of gifts ready to give away.

The recipes for preserved herbs in this chapter will be mentioned again in other chapters, as they often provide the flavor base for winter cooking. They are especially useful for those who live in colder climates where, unlike the temperate West Coast, they cannot go and pick rosemary and thyme and sage on a rainy evening just before dinner. Also, those who do not live in large cities where fresh herbs are now available in winter can use this chapter to create their own supply.

I start preserving herbs in July, and by October my supply is nearly complete. If spread over several months, this is an ongoing pleasure and never becomes an ordeal. It feels like culinary money in the bank, and is truly one of winter's pleasures. The following recipes and methods are ones I have collected and experimented with for the last ten years. They have proven to be the most flavorful and have become my favorites.

Freezing

*W*hen the tarragon, chives and mint have gone for their winter vacation and I can only scrounge the occasional hardy leaf, I turn to preserves made in August or September, when everything is still luxuriant. I always freeze bags or jars of tarragon, dill, mint, lovage, chives and lemon balm: herbs that freeze well and retain the most flavor and color, and that are not usually available in stores in darkest December.

Parsley freezes well or, in more temperate areas, it grows in the garden all winter. Parsley is always available in most supermarkets and, combined with green onions, is a reliable source of herbal flavor for cooks longing for something green to snip into their food. Cilantro freezes well in bags, and it is also usually available in winter, especially in Chinese markets.

Tarragon freezes well, but there are other methods of preservation. French chefs often buy large amounts of tarragon from us in August or September. They put it in large jars and fill it up with white vinegar.

The cook can use the leaves for flavoring and the vinegar for dressings and sauces. Tarragon can also be made into a herb paste with oil and frozen or refrigerated.

To freeze herbs, wash the freshly picked herbs well, spin them dry in a salad spinner and strip the leaves off the stalks. Package them in plastic bags or small glass jars (so they are easy to see). Snip chives in fine pieces with scissors before bagging and freezing. Dill, which should be washed very well, as it attracts bugs, can be frozen in small bouquets in plastic bags. Thaw and finely chop it for use in recipes. Lovage can be packaged in small amounts for soup or stew recipes. I put four or five leaves in a package, often leaving them on the stalk. Mint and lemon balm, frozen in half-cup (125-mL) measures in plastic bags can be added to winter sorbets, teas and custards.

Some vegetables freeze well too. I always have a glut of peppers and tomatoes in September. They are easy to freeze and delicious in winter stews and sauces. Shallots are the aristocrat of the onion family. Their sweetish, garlicky flavor and rosy purple hue make them a vital flavoring agent. Shallots will keep all winter if stored correctly in a cool airy place — we hang them in the garage in string onion bags. But frozen shallots are a special boon to the busy cook. The flavor of shallots is at its peak when first harvested, so freezing some at this time makes good culinary sense.

Frozen Puréed Sorrel

This tart, lemon-flavored, spinachlike plant adds a zip to many winter dishes. The secret of a supply of beautiful sorrel leaves is rich soil, water and not letting the plant go to seed. All summer long we whack off the sorrel seed heads, and fertilize with compost and fish fertilizer.

To prepare for the freezer, wash 4 cups (1 L) leaves, snip off the coarse stalks and place the leaves in a large saucepan. Add enough water to cover the bottom of the pan to a depth of a couple of inches (10 cm) and bring to a boil. Steam for a few minutes, until sorrel has softened and turned a drab khaki color. Drain in a colander, then purée in a food processor or blender. Freeze the purée in small plastic cartons, jars or in ice-cube trays. The ice-cube trays are handy for small amounts of sorrel flavoring — for example, in a cream sauce for fish. When frozen solid, store ice cubes in plastic bags and label. Makes about 1 cup (250 mL).

Lovage Vegetarian Stock

This lovage vegetarian stock is high in flavor for soups, stews and sauces. A plus for this stock is that it contains no fat. Makes 1 quart (1 L).

4 cups (1 L) washed lovage leaves

6 cups (1.5 L) water

freshly ground pepper

Put all ingredients in a saucepan and bring to a boil. Reduce heat and simmer for 10 minutes. Cool and put in plastic or glass containers with lids. Label and freeze. The stock can also be frozen in ice-cube trays. When frozen solid, place ice cubes in plastic bags and label.

Tarragon Paste

Use this tarragon paste in sauces for chicken or fish, in salad dressings or in soup recipes. Makes about 1 cup (250 mL).

2 cups (500 mL) tarragon leaves

1/2 cup (125 mL) oil

Pick a large bunch of tarragon. Wash well and strip leaves off the tough stalks. Spin the leaves in a salad spinner. Place in a food processor, and process until finely chopped. Add oil and continue to process to a smooth paste. Freeze in ice-cube trays or small containers.

Quick-Frozen Tomatoes

When I discovered this method of preserving tomatoes I was elated. Eliminate the guilt of tomato glut in September; do something with the tomatoes in winter when you have more time.

All you need is one large basket of ripe tomatoes you don't know what to do with, and some freezer bags. Wash the tomatoes and cut off the blemishes and blossom part. Bag them, seal with a twist tie, and pop them in the freezer.

In the winter you can take out these red bullets one at a time. Hold each tomato under hot tap-water until the skin slips off and then pop it into soups, stews or sauces. They will taste far better than store-bought canned tomatoes full of salt and preservatives. About four or five tomatoes equal a large can of stewed tomatoes in a recipe.

Tomato Purée with Garlic, Basil and Thyme

This sauce can be used as a flavor jolt to any pasta sauce, soups, gravy, meat balls, meat loaf or baked beans and chili. Makes about 4 cups (1 L).

10 ripe large tomatoes

4 cloves garlic, peeled and chopped

1/4 cup (50 mL) fresh basil

a few sprigs of thyme

freshly ground pepper

salt, if desired

Place 10 large, perfectly ripe tomatoes in a bowl. Pour boiling water over them to loosen the skins. After one minute, drain and run cold water over them. Slip the skins off the tomatoes.

Place tomatoes in a saucepan with the peeled chopped garlic, basil, thyme and pepper. Bring to a boil and simmer until very thick. Cool and freeze in small containers. If you wish to remove the seeds, put through a sieve or food mill. Vary by increasing the garlic, adding shallots or onions, or using marjoram, oregano and lovage for a herbal variation.

Freezing Peppers

I usually have too many peppers in September, but they are simple to freeze for use in winter. Wash the peppers, cut them in half and .remove the seeds and white membrane. Pop into freezer bags and seal with twist ties. In December, I often make a batch of red pepper jam (see page 96) to serve with ham and turkey. You can also purée the peppers to use in pasta or meat sauces.

The Cook's Secret Shallot Supply

A supply of shallots, all peeled and sitting in jars in the herb section of your freezer, means you have a secret ingredient that will improve many recipes. Substitute shallots for their onion cousins any time. As they can be fiddly to peel when you are in a hurry, it is pleasant to think of them in your freezer, poised to fall into a recipe.

Peel the shallots. Place in clean, clear glass jars with good lids and freeze. Baby-food jars are excellent for this. You can take out a few shallots at a time and reseal the rest.

A Cache of Garlic Purée

The garlic of summer is at its best in freshness and flavor, so this is a good time to preserve it. Use the garlic purée in bean dishes, soups, sauces, and marinades for lamb. Makes 1 cup (250 mL).

6 heads garlic, separated into cloves

3-4 Tbsp. (45-60 mL) olive oil

freshly ground pepper

Place cloves of garlic in a saucepan of water and simmer about 20 minutes until soft. Drain in a colander until cool. Peel and put in the food processor. Add the olive oil and pepper and process to a purée. Place in a small, lidded, glass jar and freeze.

Drying

I dry very few herbs as I am such a fresh herb devotée, and feel the taste and flavor of most dried herbs is minimal. Oregano dries well and retains good flavor for winter pasta sauces and pizza. Sage and savory also perform well dried, as they contain volatile oils that keep their flavor. I also dry a few herbs for teas, such as lemon verbena, lemon balm, lemon thyme, mint and camomile.

There are several ways of drying herbs. One method is to tie the herbs in bundles and hang them in the kitchen. They look beautiful, but are mainly decorative as they attract dust and insects. I look at them with pleasure but I don't cook with them. The second method is to place bunches of herbs in paper bags, close the bags with twist ties and place in a cool, dark cupboard. This is how I dry oregano and tea herbs. In November or December, remove the herbs from the bags and put the leaves in clean bottles with tight caps. The tea herbs can be placed in pretty tins you have collected. You can blend your herbal teas and make up unique names. These make charming presents for friends who like herbal teas.

You can also make sun-dried tomatoes if you're tired of freezing the excess tomatoes. They are a little fussy to do, but it's always a thrill to make your own luxury gourmet items.

Drying Herbs in an Oven

Herbs can be dried in a regular or convection oven at a very low heat (100-150°F/40-65°C) for three to five minutes. When dry, strip the leaves off the stalks and bottle in jars with tight lids. Keep for only a year, as the flavor fades.

I have done a small amount of experimenting with drying herbs in a microwave oven. Parsley and dill, microwaved at 90°F (35°C) on medium power for 1 1/2 minutes, dried well and had a good color and reasonable flavor.

It is an interesting experience to taste the dried and fresh herb, one after the other. The microwaved herb had a much weaker taste than the fresh, of course, but in the depths of winter it is better than no herb at all. I will continue to experiment with herb drying and the microwave, for it certainly is a quick and easy way of preserving herbs.

Lemon Delight Herbal Tea

Add pieces of dried lemon rind or orange rind to this tea for extra flavor, or experiment with cloves and cinnamon. The herbal tea creator has endless possibilities.

1 part dried lemon verbena leaves

1 part dried lemon thyme leaves

1 part dried lemon balm leaves

1 part dried mint leaves

Mix all the dried herbs in a bowl, then package and label.

Drying Calendula and Lavender

I sprinkle calendula petals on food all summer and they are easy to dry for winter. To dry, spread the petals out in flat wicker baskets that are available in Chinatown. In winter calendula petals can be used in rice dishes, pasta dishes or in cornbread recipes.

Lavender is a herb whose culinary uses have been neglected for years, but now there is a lavender comeback. I have recently found recipes in new cookbooks for lavender jelly as a dessert or condiment, and a lavender ice cream from the South of France.

Try flavoring honey with lavender and enjoy a new-old sensation with teatime scones or biscuits. Lavender honey is intriguing on pancakes, too. In July, pick some perfect sprigs of lavendar and insert them in small jars of honey. Set aside for a month or so to let the flavor permeate.

To make lavender sugar for use in winter baking, put some white sugar in a clean jar with a tight lid. Place eight or ten fresh lavender sprigs in the sugar and seal. Make sure the sprigs are dry. Store for a month or so to let the lavender flavor permeate. You can add extra sugar to the jar as you use it.

Lavender can be dried the same way as calendula. This aromatic herb can be tossed in green salads, put in vinegar, added to fruit salads and mixed with rosemary and fennel when barbecuing and roasting meat and fish. Small amounts of lavender can be added to cookie recipes, sorbets or custards. It has a very strong taste, so begin your lavender experiments cautiously.

Sun-dried Tomatoes with Herbs

Pear-shaped Roma Italian tomatoes are specially grown for tomato paste and are best for drying. Romas are usually ready from your garden in September and in the markets in September and October.

To prepare dried tomatoes, wash the plum tomatoes and dry with paper towel. Cut them in half, removing the coarse stem part with a knife. Sprinkle the cut part with salt and place the tomatoes on racks.

Cover the tomatoes with cheesecloth to keep the insects away and dry them in the sunlight for two or three days, depending on the weather. Bring them inside in the evening if the weather is threatening. They can always be finished off indoors if it rains.

Tomatoes can also be dried in a dehydrator, a regular oven or a convection oven. I have used the convection oven and found it very satisfactory. The preparation is the same no matter which method you use to dry the tomatoes. My small convection oven did a perfect job in about eight hours.

To dry tomatoes in the oven, set the convection oven at 200°F (95°C) and leave the door slightly ajar. Dry about six to eight hours, until tomatoes are leathery and dried up like prunes. Cool.

Swish dried tomatoes in a bowl of vinegar. Lay the tomatoes on a paper towel and pat them dry. Put the dried tomatoes in sterilized jars and cover well with olive oil. At this time you can add sprigs of rosemary, sage or winter savory. Screw cap on well, label and refrigerate, or put them in the proverbial dark cupboard.

In my sun-dried tomato research I found one book that suggested you could preserve your sun-dried tomatoes by putting the filled jars in a boiling water bath for 15 minutes. Mine have been fine in the refrigerator and they do not last long, for I slip these little red flavor concentrates into stews, soups and pastas. They add a richness that Italian cooks have known about for hundreds of years.

Preserving Basil

I do not like dried basil. Eleven years of experimenting with basil preservation has resulted in other methods that best preserve the flavor. When frozen in bags, the flavor is quite good, but it darkens, so only use it in a soup or sauce. Frozen in olive oil, basil retains its green color and its flavor. Pesto is a flavorful way of preserving basil. After reading many Italian cookbooks, I tried storing pesto in the refrigerator for the winter, in a sterilized jar, covered with a slick of oil and a lid. This method can work, with care (keeping well sealed in a sterilized container), but for extra insurance, pesto can always be frozen. When refrigerating, always put an extra slick of oil on top after spooning some out, or it will darken.

Basil Oil Ice Cubes

Drop one or two of these cubes into a soup or spaghetti sauce and your dish will have that real basil boost. Makes about 1-2 cups (250-500 mL).

2 cups (500 mL) fresh basil leaves, packed

1/2 cup (125 mL) olive oil or any light oil

Wash the bunches of basil and spin dry in a salad spinner. Remove coarse stems. Place in a food processor or blender. Process until puréed, then slowly add the oil and process to a smooth paste. Put immediately into ice-cube trays, cover trays tightly with plastic wrap and freeze. When frozen solid, remove cubes and store in a plastic bag.

Basil Preserved in Parmesan Cheese

I found this recipe in a charming little cookbook called Recipes From a Kitchen Garden *from Shepherd's Garden Seeds in California. This company is a great source of various basil seeds and exotic greens, lettuces and vegetables. This is a variation on the Italian refrigerator method. Makes 2 cups (500 mL).*

2 cups (500 mL) tightly packed, washed and spun dry basil leaves

1 cup (250 mL) freshly grated Parmesan cheese or asiago cheese

salt, pepper and olive oil.

Finely mince basil leaves. Put in a large bowl and add the cheese. Mix well.

Sprinkle salt and pepper in the bottom of a sterilized 2-cup (500-mL) jar with a tight lid. Add 1/2 inch (1 cm) of basil/cheese mix. Press down. Sprinkle with salt and pepper. Add another layer of basil cheese mix, salt and pepper and 1/4 inch (.6 cm) of oil. Continue until the jar is full. Top the jar with 1/4 inch (.6 cm) of olive oil. Seal. Refrigerate and use as needed; with care, it will keep until next year's basil crop is ready.

Basil Pesto

Basil pesto is now firmly entrenched as a summer classic, but it freezes well and you can enjoy it all winter on pasta or crackers and added to soups and sauces for increased flavor. Makes 2 cups (500 mL).

2 cups (500 mL) freshly washed, firmly packed basil leaves

2-4 cloves garlic, peeled and crushed

1/2 cup (125 mL) olive or vegetable oil

3 Tbsp. (45 mL) pine nuts

1 cup (250 mL) freshly grated Parmesan cheese

Put basil and garlic in a blender or food processor. Pour in oil and process until smooth. Add pine nuts and process for a few seconds. Stir in Parmesan cheese. If sauce is too thick, add more oil. Store in a jar in the refrigerator with a skim of oil on top and cover with plastic wrap.

To freeze, place pesto in plastic cartons and label. Thaw slowly at room temperature. If desired, omit pine nuts and cheese when processing. Add them to the thawed pesto just before serving for fresh taste.

Infinite Pesto Variations

*P*esto is a herb paste and is derived from the word "pestle." Purists still make it in a mortar and pestle, but do not feel guilty about using a food processor — it does a wonderful job.

After a year or so of only making basil pestos, I started to experiment with cilantro, tarragon and mint. I tried different nuts, such as sunflower seeds, walnuts or almonds, and substituted canola or safflower oil for olive oil.

Using your imagination and your herb garden, you can make sorrel, fennel, chives, lemon thyme, and a variety of vegetable pestos. Even the powerful herbs such as rosemary and sage can be used as accent notes with spinach and parsley. Explore and experiment. Pestos are an excellent flavoring agent for so many dishes — a back-up supply in the freezer and refrigerator is magic for the cook.

In winter you can make a pesto with spinach and parsley, which are always available, and add garlic, cheese, nuts, shallots and green onions. I prefer not to use dried herbs in pestos as I do not like the taste. The following recipes may be used fresh, refrigerated or frozen.

Pestos may be kept in the refrigerator for varying lengths of time. They should always have a slick of oil on top and be tightly covered with plastic wrap to keep all air out.

Tarragon Pesto

Tarragon's aniselike, smoky flavor is quite unique. Use it with pasta or as a quick fish sauce, or add a dollop to a salad dressing. Makes 1 cup (50 mL).

1 1/2 cups (750 mL) fresh tarragon leaves

1/2 cup (125 mL) fresh parsley leaves

3 whole cloves garlic, peeled

1/2 cup (125 mL) olive oil

1/2 cup (125 mL) pine nuts

1/2 cup (125 mL) Parmesan cheese, grated

freshly ground pepper

Put tarragon, parsley and garlic in the processor. Process briefly. Pour in oil slowly while machine is running. Add nuts, cheese and pepper and process for a few seconds. Cover with plastic wrap and refrigerate or freeze.

Cilantro Pesto

Besides the usual uses with pasta, spoon this mysterious-flavored sauce over vegetables and fish, use it in a yogurt dip for fresh vegetables, or stuff it under the skin of a whole chicken or chicken breasts. Makes about 1 cup (250 mL).

2 cups (500 mL) fresh cilantro leaves

2-4 cloves garlic, peeled

1/2 cup (125 mL) fresh grated Parmesan or asiago cheese

3 Tbsp. (45 mL) pine nuts or sunflower seeds

1/2 cup (125 mL) olive oil

freshly ground pepper

dash of cayenne pepper

Put cilantro leaves, garlic, cheese and nuts in the food processor and process. Slowly add oil while the machine is running. Add pepper and cayenne. If it is too thick, add a little more oil.

Mint Pesto

At Ravenhill Farm we raise lamb, and mint pesto is the condiment for roast lamb, lamb chops or barbecued lamb. Makes about 1 cup (250 mL).

2 cups (500 mL) fresh mint leaves

2-4 cloves garlic, peeled

1/4 cup (50 mL) freshly grated Parmesan cheese

1/4 cup (50 mL) pine nuts or sunflower seeds

1/2 cup (125 mL) olive oil

freshly ground pepper

Process the mint, garlic, cheese and nuts in a food processor. With the machine running, slowly add the oil. Add the pepper.

Herb Jellies

erb jellies have the two important qualities that please cooks: they taste delicious and they look beautiful. I like to look at the pale, jewellike colors — the pink of rosemary, the pale yellow of lemon thyme and the vivid green of mint. Simple to make, herb jellies are one of the most satisfying products you can create from your herb garden. I make rosemary, sage, mint, basil, lemon thyme and lemon balm. More than one herb can be combined and other ingredients may be added, such as apples, crab apples, cranberries, lemons and oranges. The cook as artist has a unique opportunity to flower when making jellies. Choosing the herb, the jar, and the labeling all go into making a little jar of edible art, and the jelly lasts a lot longer than a plate of food elegantly displayed. The book *Fancy Pantry*, by Helen Witty, will inspire the jelly maker to greater heights.

Herb jellies are basically savory, but are very good on scones, bagels, muffins, crumpets and toast. They are delicious with all kinds of meat and poultry. I baste chicken with rosemary jelly and often add a spoonful to pan juices and gravy for extra flavor. For a brunch or tea party, set out three or four herb jellies. They add a charming decorative touch to your table.

When making a herb jelly, essentially you are making a jelly from a herbal tea. Sometimes, I do confess, I add a drop or two of food coloring — red for rosemary, green for mint and yellow for sage and tarragon — for herb teas can be somewhat drab in color. You can also use red wine vinegar to increase the red color. I often put sprigs of the herb in the jelly just before I seal the jar, for a pretty effect.

Master Herb Jelly Recipe

You can use this as a master recipe for all your herb jellies. As you become more experienced with jelly making, you can change the recipe to suit your palate. Makes 4 cups (1 L).

1-2 cups (250-500 mL) washed and chopped herb (use the lesser amount for rosemary and sage, as they have strong volatile oils)

1 1/4 cups (300 mL) boiling water

1/4 cup (50 mL) white wine vinegar

3 cups (750 mL) white sugar

2 Tbsp. (30 mL) fresh lemon juice

2-3 drops of food coloring (optional)

1/2 bottle of liquid pectin

sprigs of fresh herbs (optional)

Put the chopped herbs in a saucepan and pour the boiling water over them. Let sit for 15-20 minutes. The herbs release more flavor if they are chopped and if they steep for at least 15 minutes.

Strain the herb liquid through a coffee filter or cheesecloth into another saucepan. Add the vinegar, sugar and lemon juice and bring to a boil, stirring well to dissolve the sugar. Add food coloring, if desired, and pectin. Stir constantly for one minute. Remove from heat. Skim foam off mixture, and pour into hot sterilized jars. Put a sprig of the herb in the jelly at this time if desired. Seal the jars with paraffin wax or canning lids. Label and store.

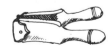

Vinegars

*M*y kitchen is decorated with herbal and fruit vinegars. The bright red of opal basil, the yellowish green of tarragon, the pale pink of chive flowers, the deeper green of dill and the rosy red of raspberry all add gay hits of color to the kitchen. Herbal vinegars are not difficult to make, once you have rounded up your equipment and supplies. I use large glass jars I get from a friendly delicatessen. Large mayonnaise or pickle jars from restaurants can also be used. The vinegars sit in these containers until I am ready to bottle them.

For vinegar, I prefer California wine vinegar. It has more taste and is less harsh than distilled vinegar. I buy it in bulk from a restaurant food wholesaler (check your yellow pages). One case contains four 3-quart (3-litre) bottles of red or white wine vinegar. This is a lot of vinegar for one household, so share it with some friends. Remember that vinegar keeps, so it will not go to waste.

The search for bottles for vinegar is an ongoing enjoyable task. I look in second-hand stores for unique old bottles and in kitchen shops for pretty Italian bottles with clusters of grapes on the side. Be sure they have plasticized screw caps as the vinegar attacks corks and metal.

Labeling is the next artistic task. If you are talented with a calligraphy pen you can make your own labels with a countrified air. There are very pretty labels available now in kitchen and gift shops which will make your bottles of vinegar very decorative. This is one of the many pleasures of being a domestic sensualist.

There are many uses for herbal and fruit vinegars: making salad vinaigrettes, marinating meat and chicken, flavoring vegetables, adding to meat and chicken sauces, and adding to seafood sautées, pasta salads, barbecue sauces, chili sauces, and chutney and pickle recipes, to name a few. In any recipe that calls for regular vinegar, substitute one of your own vinegars and you will improve the flavor.

I like the sweet fruit vinegars on more robust greens, such as arugula, spinach, and cabbage. The herb vinegars go into dressings for milder, more delicate lettuces.

Some books suggest leaving the vinegars in the sun and others recommend a dark cupboard. The sun tends to fade flower vinegar, such as chive and nasturtium, but the vinegar bottles do look wonderful sitting in the window. I like to have a rest after vinegar making and gaze at them.

Herbal Vinegars

I make herbal vinegars all summer long in the big glass jars. Dill, lovage, tarragon, green and opal basil, lemon thyme, bay leaves, and oregano all work well; in fact you are only limited by what is growing in your herb garden and your time and energy.

September is usually bottling month and then I create interesting combinations. Italian Garden Vinegar contains basil, a peeled garlic clove and some sprigs of Italian parsley or fennel. French Garden has a peeled shallot, a sprig of thyme and a bay leaf. Lemon Delight has lemon balm, lemon thyme, lemon verbena and a sliver of lemon rind. Salad Delight has a garlic clove, a bay leaf and some dill. The possibilities for the cook-artist-gardener are endless, and your winter salads and sauces will have a sprightly lift that tastes a lot better than a commercial dressing.

There are two methods for making the herb vinegars: hot and cold. For the hot method, heat the vinegar in a large pot just to the boiling point. Sterilize the bottles. Poke three or four well-washed sprigs of herb into the bottles. Using a funnel, pour the heated vinegar into the bottle, leaving a ¼-inch (.6 cm) space, and cap tightly. The theory behind heating the vinegar is that it brings out a more intense herb flavor.

For the cold method, pour the cold vinegar into sterilized bottles that have the herb inserted in them. The herb flavor will take a few weeks to permeate the vinegar.

Fruit Vinegars

Starting in June and July, fill a few sterilized crocks with strawberries, raspberries and, in August, blackberries. Pour wine vinegar over the fruit and cover well to keep out dust and bugs. Allow the fruit and vinegar to sit for several weeks or a couple of months. The vinegar will become more fruit-flavored every day.

After a minimum of three weeks soaking, filter the vinegar through a coffee filter or several layers of cheesecloth. This gives the vinegar a clear color that looks enticing. Place in sterilized bottles and cap tightly. You can pop one or two berries in the bottles just before you cap them.

If you freeze berries for the winter, you can make fruit vinegars in December. Simply put the frozen berries in a sterilized crock or glass jar and let steep for a few weeks, following the same method.

Flower Vinegars

Nasturtium flowers make a beautiful orange-red vinegar with a peppery flavor. Wash the flowers carefully and spin dry in the salad spinner. Never use flowers that have been sprayed with insecticides. Place 2-3 cups (500-750 mL) of nasturtiums in a large glass jar with about 1 quart (1 L) of vinegar. Cover and let steep for a month or so. Strain through a coffee filter or layers of cheesecloth and then bottle. You can use a mixture of herb flowers, such as chive, borage, lemon thyme, fennel mint, violets and roses. Flower vinegars are subtle and delicate, so when making salad dressings use a light vegetable oil like safflower oil. Rice vinegar is a good base, as it is lighter in flavor than wine vinegars.

Herbal Oils

*H*erbal oils add a new dimension to salad dressings, mayonnaises, sautéeing, frying and baking. Pizza restaurants in the South of France always have a bottle of herbed olive oil stuffed with rosemary, thyme and peppercorns on the table to drizzle over your pizza.

Strong-tasting herbs and olive oil make the best herbal combination. Rosemary is my favorite, and basil, garlic, marjoram, oregano and thyme are also very good.

You can make a large amount in a quart (litre) bottle. The herbs should be clean, but not wet from washing, when you put them into the bottles. Spin the herbs dry in a salad spinner and pat with paper towels. Put a least two cups (500 mL) of herbs in the bottle. Twist and bruise them a little to release the flavors. Fill the bottle with oil. Cover and store in a cool place for a few weeks of steeping.

I do not make vast amounts of herbal oil at once and I try to use it up quickly. It will keep for a year, but sometimes it gets cloudy and murky as it responds to temperature changes.

Pickles and Preserves

*Q*uick and delicious perfectly describe these two recipes, which can add a lift to winter meals. The pickled shallots are crisp and sweet and the zucchini relish is a versatile condiment.

Pickled Shallots

Recipes for pickled shallots are found in many old English cookbooks. I have a copy of Mrs. Beeton's Jam Making and Preserves and Pickles *in my collection of old cookbooks and her recipe for pickled shallots is somewhat intimidating, as it takes eight days, in all. The following recipe takes less time and produces a ladylike, subtle, crunchy pickle. They are delicious with a grilled cheese sandwich or as a condiment for a cold buffet supper. Makes 4 cups (1 L).*

16 shallots, peeled

1 Tbsp. (15 mL) salt

1 cup (250 mL) malt vinegar or herb-flavored wine vinegar

1 Tbsp. (15 mL) brown sugar

1 small bunch dill

Place the shallots in a bowl, add salt and cover with water. Refrigerate overnight, to crisp.

The next morning drain the shallots, put them in a saucepan, add vinegar and sugar and boil for about five minutes. Allow to cool before placing in a sterilized jar. Poke the washed dill well into the vinegar. Cap with a tight-fitting lid and refrigerate. Allow a few weeks to develop a good pickled flavor before using.

Zucchini Freezer Relish with Basil

This peppy, herby relish is a perfect companion for hamburgers, hot dogs, cold cuts and meat loaf. A vegetarian friend puts it on her tofu. Frozen in attractive small jars, it makes a nice gift. The relish is a sprightly yellow with green flecks. Makes 12 cups (3 L).

5 lbs. (2 1/2 kg) zucchini

6 large onions

1/2 cup (125 mL) coarse pickling salt

2 cups (500 mL) white wine vinegar (your own herb-flavored one preferably)

2 tsp. (10 mL) dry mustard

3 tsp. (15 mL) celery seed

1 tsp. (5 mL) *each* cinnamon, nutmeg and pepper

1 Tbsp. (15 mL) turmeric

1 cup (250 mL) finely chopped basil

2 Tbsp. (30 mL) finely chopped marjoram or oregano

Cut zucchini and onion in large chunks and process until finely chopped but not mashed. Put in a large bowl with the salt. Cover with water and refrigerate overnight.

The next day, drain the vegetables and rinse with cold water. Put the vegetables in a large saucepan with all the rest of the ingredients, except the chopped herbs. Bring to a boil, stirring constantly. Reduce to a simmer and cook for 20 to 30 minutes. The relish should be quite thick. This might take longer as there are so many variables, such as stoves, size of pots and amounts. Remove from heat and add the chopped herbs. Cool the relish and put in sterilized jars, leaving an inch (2.5 cm) or so at the top for expansion. Cap, label and freeze.

CHAPTER TWO

Baking with Herbs

One of my great passions is making bread, buns and biscuits. I began nearly thirty years ago. I was living in a cottage on the sea with a small child who loved my bread failures, for then we could go out on the deck and feed the seagulls. Determined to make truly wonderful bread, I persisted. Slowly the bread improved and the seagulls lost part of their staple diet, for people had eaten it all.

Starting the herb farm caused a felicitous marriage between bread baking and herb growing. I now put herbs in most of my baking — in French bread, whole-wheat rolls, biscuits, soda bread, and, yes, even in Yorkshire pudding. My favorite baking herbs are rosemary and sage, but I also use chervil, chives, basil and lovage. My basic French bread recipe has evolved over thirty years. Sometimes the herbs go inside and sometimes only on top.

Making bread is a happy and sensuous experience that makes gloomy winter days more cheery. Kneading bread can ease depression and frustration, as well as strengthen your upper body muscles. The smell of herbs and baking bread is truly a perfume for kitchen gods and goddesses.

Pesto Bread

Pesto and bread are staples at Ravenhill Herb Farm, and it seemed a natural conclusion to combine them. This interesting, small, round loaf is golden brown outside and the palest green inside. I made it for a basil cooking class, in which I was attempting to put basil into everything. Use freshly made pesto or pesto you have frozen or stored in the refrigerator. Other pestos, such as cilantro, or parsley tarragon, would make interesting herb breads. My inspiration for pesto bread and other Italian baking comes from Carol Field's Italian Baking. *She traveled all over Italy looking for regional recipes and the resulting book is an education in Italian bread baking. Makes 2 loaves.*

1/2 cup (125mL) pesto sauce (recipes page 13-15)

2 1/2 tsp. (12 mL) dry yeast

1 cup (250mL) warm water

2 Tbsp. (25 mL) olive oil

3 3/4 cups (925 mL) unbleached all-purpose flour

2 tsp. (10 mL) salt

Have pesto sauce ready. Mix yeast with the warm water in a mixing bowl. Let stand for ten minutes until bubbly. Add oil and pesto sauce. Stir until mixed. Add flour and salt and mix well. Knead dough on a floured surface until it is a soft, smooth, pale green ball. Lightly oil the dough, place in an oiled bowl and let rise until doubled in size, about 1 1/2 hours.

Punch down and shape into two rounded loaves. Place seam side down on a cookie sheet sprinkled with cornmeal. Cover with a clean cloth. Let rise about 45 minutes, until almost doubled in size.

Heat oven to 450°F (230°C). Put the bread in the oven and reduce heat to 400°F (200°C). With a water sprayer, spray into the oven about three times in the first ten minutes, to help make a crisper crust. Bake about 35-40 minutes. (Note: if making pesto buns rather than loaves, bake buns for about 30 minutes.) Cool on racks.

Foccacia

This flattish, chewy, herb- and salt-laced snack bread is another of Italy's gifts to culinary art. The following is a basic foccacia recipe, with a variety of toppings. My favorite is rosemary and coarse sea salt or chopped shallots. Makes 3 round, 9-inch (23-cm) loaves.

3 tsp. (15 mL) dry yeast

1/4 cup (50 mL) warm water

2 1/4 cups (500 mL) warm water

2 Tbsp. (30 mL) olive oil

2-4 Tbsp. (30-60 mL) freshly chopped rosemary or sage (1-2 Tbsp/ 15-30 mL dried may be substituted)

7 1/2 cups (1.875 L) unbleached all-purpose flour

1 Tbsp (15 mL) coarse salt

1 cup (250 mL) chopped onions, garlic, olives, and herbs of choice

Mix yeast and 1/4 cup (50 mL) warm water in a large bowl. Let yeast develop and bubble for ten minutes. Add the 2 1/4 cups (550 mL) water, olive oil and freshly chopped rosemary or sage. Add two cups (500 mL) of the flour and mix well. Add the rest of the flour gradually until the dough becomes firm enough to knead.

Knead dough on a floured surface for at least ten minutes, until it forms a smooth, nonsticky ball. Place in a bowl oiled with olive oil, lightly oil the top of the bread and let rise until doubled in size, about 1 1/2 hours.

Punch down and divide into three smooth, flat rounds. Place on greased pie plates and let rise for about half an hour. Dimple the dough by poking 1/2-inch-deep (1-cm) holes in the top with oiled fingertips. These holes make little caves for the oil, salt and herbs to nestle in. Cover with a cloth and let rise another hour and a half.

Sprinkle the foccacia with coarse salt and chopped onions, garlic, olives, herbs or a combination of toppings. Brush very generously with olive oil. Place in a 400°F (200°C) oven and spray water into the oven with a water sprayer a couple of times in the first 5-10 minutes. Bake 20-25 minutes. Cool on racks. Serve on a bread board, surrounded by sprigs of herbs. Some books advise against storing it in the refrigerator, but usually foccacia does not last until the next day.

Fougasse

In Provence a few years ago I discovered fougasse, the French cousin of foccacia bread. It makes a wonderful picnic lunch with olives and cheese. All you need is a hillside with a view, a glass of wine and a good companion. Makes 4 loaves.

3 tsp. (15 mL) dried yeast

1/4 cup (50 mL) warm water

7 cups (1.75 L) unbleached white flour

2 cups (500 mL) warm water

4 Tbsp. (60 mL) olive oil

2 tsp. (10 mL) salt

1 cup (250 mL) well-cooked crisp bacon bits

1 egg

1 Tbsp. (15 mL) water.

Combine yeast and the 1/4 cup (50 mL) warm water and let rise for about ten minutes. In a large bowl place 6 cups (1.5 L) of the flour. Stir in the water, the bubbling yeast, the olive oil and the salt. Mix well with a wooden spoon. Mix in the bacon bits. Turn dough out on a floured surface using the final cup (250 mL) of flour and knead for ten minutes, until it is smooth and does not stick to the counter. Oil dough, place in an oiled bowl and let rise for two or three hours.

Punch down and divide into four flat ovals. Place the ovals on a greased baking sheet and let rise for one hour. Cut six slashes on each oval and stretch the slashes apart with oiled fingers. Beat together the egg and water and brush on tops of loaves. Bake in a 400°F (200°C) oven for 40 minutes. Put a pan of water in the bottom of the oven to make a good crust.

Basic French Bread Recipe

You can set this bread to rise, go off for several hours and then come home and finish it. Often I set it to rise in the morning and bake it right before dinner. The secret for leaving the bread is to let it rise in a cool place (65°F/18°C). The longer the rise, the better the bread. Makes 2 loaves.

1/2 cup (125 mL) warm water

1 tsp. (5 mL) sugar

1/4 tsp. (1 mL) ginger (this is a yeast improver)

2 Tbsp. (30 mL) dry yeast

5 cups (1.25 L) unbleached white flour

2 cups (500 mL) warm water

2 Tbsp. (30 mL) sugar

1 1/2 tsp. (7 mL) salt

2 Tbsp. (25 mL) olive oil

1/4 cup (50 mL) finely chopped sage, rosemary or herb of your choice (optional)

1 cup (250 mL) flour

1 egg, beaten

1 Tbsp. (15 mL) water

chopped herbs of choice, as garnish

Combine the water, 1 tsp. (5 mL) sugar, ginger and yeast in a bowl and let stand until bubbling well, about 10 minutes. Place the 5 cups (1.25 L) flour in a large mixing bowl, and make a well in the middle of the flour. Put the 2 cups (500 mL) warm water, the bubbling yeast mixture and the 2 Tbsp. (25 mL) sugar in the depression. Mix enough flour into the yeast mixture to slightly thicken it. Let stand for about 20 minutes. The yeast mixture will mound up and bubble in the center.

Add the salt and oil and stir in the rest of the flour in the bowl.

(If you are adding the optional herbs to the inside of the loaf, add them with the oil and salt.) Mix well with a wooden spoon; the dough will be stiff.

Put the last cup (250 mL) of flour on a smooth surface and turn out the dough. Knead firmly and with energy for ten minutes. Set the timer so you do not cheat. When done, the dough should form a smooth, nonsticky ball. Lightly oil the bowl and the dough and replace the dough in the bowl. Cover with a clean cloth and let rise for at least two hours, until doubled in size.

Punch down, let rise again for another hour until doubled. Punch down, return to a floured surface and divide into two balls. Stretch each ball out flat and roll into round or long tapered loaves. Place on cookie sheets that are sprinkled with cornmeal. Let rise until almost doubled, about 40 minutes.

Preheat oven to 450°F(230°C). To make a good crust, place a pan of water in the bottom of the oven. Beat the egg with 1 Tbsp. (15 mL) water and brush the loaves with the egg wash. Using a sharp knife, make slashes across the bread at an angle. Sprinkle the loaf with chopped rosemary, sage or other herbs (or vary with sesame, poppy, caraway or celery seeds). Place the bread immediately in the hot oven.

Within the first three minutes, spray water into the oven (a few squirts from a plant sprayer filled with water will do). Bake for 45 minutes. If it is getting too brown, lower the heat to 350°F (180°C).

When the bread is done, place it on racks to cool. This bread freezes well. To serve, just wrap in foil and heat for 20 minutes at 400°F (200°C).

Whole-Wheat Bread

Using the same recipe, exchange 2 cups (500 mL) whole-wheat for 2 cups (500 mL) white flour. Shape into round or long loaves, or use ordinary loaf pans.

Petit Pain Rolls

Make wonderful breakfast rolls, or shape the dough into hamburger or hot-dog buns. Using the same basic dough recipe, shape into 4-inch (10-cm) rolls. Let rise 30 to 40 minutes. Just before putting in the oven, cut a slash on the top of each roll. Brush with the egg wash and sprinkle with seeds, chopped sage, or rosemary. Reduce baking time to about 30 minutes. Makes about 12 large rolls.

Giant Herbed Bread

Make the basic bread recipe, adding the herb you want with the oil and salt. For extra flavor, add chopped shallots and garlic sautéed in a little olive oil at this point. Shape into one large round loaf or put into a well-oiled bundt pan.

When it has risen, brush dough with the egg wash, sprinkle some chopped herbs on top and bake for 45 minutes in a 400-450°F (200-230°C) oven. If you bake the bread in a bundt pan, you can place a bouquet of herbs in the center for decoration. This is very pretty for a Sunday brunch or a picnic barbecue.

Bruschetta

If you have leftover bread from the previous recipe, this is a divine way to use it up. In the purest circumstances the bread should be grilled over a wood fire (a bistro in Seattle grills it over apple wood) but it is very simple to make at home. Just toast sliced French bread under the broiler, on a barbecue or in the toaster. Rub the toast with a peeled, cut, slightly crushed clove of garlic, sprinkle with pepper and drizzle with olive oil. Serve immediately, while it is still hot. Try topping the bruschetta with chopped, cooked tomatoes after it is grilled. Drizzle the olive oil on top of the tomatoes. Serve with a glass of wine as a simple but delicious appetizer, or with soup and salad for a light meal.

Herbed Yorkshire Pudding

As Andrew, the growing half of Ravenhill Farm, is from York-shire, there had to be a Yorkshire pudding recipe included in this section. His mother made them for dessert and they put golden syrup on the pudding. This version has herbs added and could be eaten for breakfast, brunch or with a roast at dinner. The herbs add a new touch to an old favorite. Serves 6-8.

1 1/3 cups (325 mL) all-purpose flour

1/2 tsp. (2 mL) salt

3 large eggs, well beaten

1 1/2 cups (375 mL) milk

1 Tbsp. (15 mL) chopped parsley

1 Tbsp. (15 mL) chopped thyme or lemon thyme

1 Tbsp. (15 mL) chopped rosemary

1/3 cup (75 mL) vegetable oil

Preheat oven to 400°F (200°C). Put flour and salt in a mixing bowl. Stir in the beaten eggs. Slowly pour in the milk. Add chopped herbs. Beat with a whisk until smooth. Allow to rest for 15-20 minutes.

Put the oil in a 9-inch by 13-inch (29-cm by 40-cm) baking pan or into muffin tins, and heat it in the oven for about 8 minutes. Pour the batter into the hot oiled pan and bake 40-45 minutes, or fill muffin cups 2/3 full and bake 25-30 minutes. Serve at once.

Pizza

Nutritionists have called pizza the complete food. It is a very satisfying winter food and you can flavor it with all the herbs and pestos you have tucked away. Deciding on toppings can be a creative, artistic act. Try whole sautéed garlic cloves, chopped shallots, goat's cheese and sage, ricotta, Parmesan cheese, rosemary, eggplant, anchovies, steamed broccoli, artichoke hearts, pesto, and red, green and yellow peppers. Sometimes I put dollops of pesto on the pizza just as I take it out of the oven. The following recipe is a good basic pizza dough. You can experiment with it and add small amounts of whole grain flours to change the texture. Makes 2 12-inch (30-cm) pizzas.

2 1/2 tsp. (12.5 mL) dry yeast

1 Tbsp. (15 mL) sugar

1/4 cup (50 mL) warm water

3 1/4 cups (800 mL) unbleached all-purpose flour

1 tsp. (5 mL) salt

3 Tbsp. (45 mL) olive oil

1 Tbsp. (15 mL) milk

1/2 cup (125 mL) warm water

2 Tbsp. (30 mL) very finely chopped herbs (optional)

assorted toppings

Mix the yeast, sugar, 1/4 cup (50 mL) water and 1/4 cup (50 mL) of the flour together in a bowl and set aside for ten minutes until bubbly. Put the remaining flour and salt in a mixing bowl. Make a hole in the center and pour in the yeast mixture, the olive oil, milk, water and herbs, if desired. Mix well with a wooden spoon until dough forms a ball. Place on a floured surface and knead for ten minutes. When it is smooth and elastic, place in an oiled bowl, cover with a cloth and let rise until doubled in size, about two hours.

Punch down and let rise until doubled again, about 45 minutes. Preheat oven to 450-500°F (225-250°C). Roll out the pizza dough on a floured surface. It should not be more than 1/4 inch (.6 cm) thick. Transfer dough to pan. Quickly add your toppings and brush the edges of the crust with olive oil before baking. Bake for 12-15 minutes.

Savory Herbed Oatcakes

I first had oatcakes twenty years ago while staying in a small fishing hotel in Scotland on the River Tay. At every meal there was a tin of oatcakes on the table. Elizabeth David in her epic work on bread, English Bread and Yeast Cookery, *tells how oatcakes were the staple food of Scottish and Yorkshire peasants and miners. Recipes for oatcakes came to Canada in the nineteenth century with Scottish immigrants and there are many variations. My version adds chopped thyme, sage or rosemary to the dough. It makes a crisp, chewy, savory biscuit, good with cheese, honey or jam. As an added bonus, the oats are very good for you. Makes about 20 oatcakes.*

4 cups (1 L) rolled oats (not the instant kind)

1 tsp. (5 mL) salt

3 Tbsp. (45 mL) butter, margarine or vegetable shortening

2 Tbsp. (30 mL) finely chopped herbs (rosemary, sage or thyme)

1/2 cup (125 mL) warm water, approximately

Preheat oven to 350°F (175°C). Place all ingredients except the water in the food processor and mix, using the pulse setting (or mix by hand). Slowly add warm water until the dough forms a sticky ball. Roll out on a floured board to about 1/8 of an inch (3 mm) thick. Cut in squares or rounds and place on an ungreased cookie sheet. Prick well and bake 15-20 minutes, until light brown. Cool on a rack. These can be frozen and brought out for a Scottish guest for tea.

Sage Cornmeal Bread

Cornbread has been a North American staple for several hundred years, ever since the native North Americans introduced corn to the first European immigrants. Intrepid pioneer women in covered wagons made it in a skillet and called it "journey cake." My grandmother made it on Saturna Island in the early 1900s. As a child, one of my favorite food memories is walking home from school in northern Vancouver Island, soaked by a winter coastal rain, and opening the kitchen door and smelling Johnny Cake baking for tea. Serve this chunky pungent cornbread with baked beans or chili.

1 cup (250 mL) all-purpose flour

1 cup (250 mL) cornmeal

1 Tbsp. (15 mL) baking powder

1/2 cup (125 mL) melted butter or margarine

1 cup (250 mL) milk

1 egg

1/2 cup (125 mL) frozen corn niblets

1 Tbsp. (15 mL) finely chopped sage

Preheat oven to 375°F (190°C). Mix flour, cornmeal and baking powder together. In another bowl mix butter or margarine, milk and egg together. Mix the liquid mixture into the dry. Stir until just blended. Stir in corn niblets and sage. Place in a greased 8-inch (20-cm) square pan and bake for about 20 minutes. The top should be golden brown. Serve warm.

Cilantro Corn Muffins

The variety in cornbread recipes is amazing. Southern recipes often include chilies. My favorites have herbs. Baked beans, chili and soup all go well with cornbread. Makes 12 muffins.

3 1/3 cups (825 mL) cornmeal

1 1/4 cups (300 mL) milk

1 cup (250 mL) all-purpose flour

3 tsp. (15 mL) baking powder

sprinkle of salt

1/3 cup (75 mL) sugar

1 egg, beaten

1/4 cup (50 mL) vegetable oil

1 tsp. (5 mL) dried crumbled chilies

4 Tbsp. (60 mL) chopped cilantro

Preheat oven to 400°F (200°C). Grease 12 muffin cups. Mix the cornmeal with the milk and set aside for five minutes.

In a large bowl, mix the flour, baking powder, salt and sugar. Add the egg, oil, chilies and cilantro to the cornmeal and milk mixture. Combine the wet and dry mixtures and stir until just blended. Spoon into a muffin pan and bake for 20 minutes.

Rosemary Beer Bread

This recipe is quick, easy and impressive. Makes 1 loaf.

3 cups (750 mL) self-rising flour

2 Tbsp. (25 mL) sugar

1/2 cup (125 mL) freshly grated Parmesan cheese

1 Tbsp. (15 mL) finely chopped rosemary

1 can or bottle of beer

1 tsp. (5 mL) melted butter or margarine

In a large bowl, mix flour, sugar, Parmesan cheese and rosemary. Stir in the beer until the flour is just moistened. Pour batter into a greased 9-inch by 5-inch (23-cm by 13-cm) loaf pan and let sit for thirty minutes, to allow the yeast in the beer to work.

Preheat oven to 350°F (175°C). Bake loaf for one hour. Remove from the oven and brush top with melted butter or margarine. Allow to sit for five minutes before removing from pan to cool on a rack.

Dill Baking-Powder Biscuits

Use some frozen dill you have preserved in September, or substitute frozen chopped chives or chopped parsley, which is always available. These biscuits are quick to make and cook and are a nice surprise for a luxurious Sunday breakfast when your friends only expected toast. Makes 12 biscuits.

2 cups (500 mL) all-purpose flour

4 tsp. (20 mL) baking powder

1/4 cup (50 mL) vegetable shortening, margarine or butter

3/4 cup (175 mL) milk

1 Tbsp. (15 mL) dill seed

1/2 cup (125 mL) finely chopped frozen dill leaves

Preheat oven to 400°F (200°C). Sift flour and baking powder together. Cut in shortening and mix with a knife or fingers until mixture is the consistency of cornmeal. Add milk, dill seed and dill. Stir until a soft dough is formed.

On a floured surface, knead dough lightly a few times. Roll out to 1/2 inch (1.2 cm) thick and cut into rounds with a floured cutter. Bake for 12-15 minutes. Serve hot. (You can vary these biscuits with the stronger flavors of rosemary and sage and serve them with soup and stew.)

Winter Savory Stilton Biscuits

Robust Stilton cheese pairs well with the peppery, piny flavor of winter savory. Makes 15-18 biscuits.

3 Tbsp. (45 mL) finely chopped winter savory

2 cups (500 mL) all-purpose flour

2 tsp. (10 mL) baking powder

1/2 tsp. (2.5 mL) baking soda

1 cup (250 mL) grated Stilton cheese, or substitute sharp
   Cheddar or blue cheese

1/2 cup (125 mL) butter or margarine

1 tsp. (5 mL) sugar

1 large egg

2/3 cup (150 mL) buttermilk

Preheat oven to 400°F (200°C). Mix savory and dry ingredients in a bowl with the cheese. Mix in butter or margarine with your fingers until it looks like fine cornmeal. Mix sugar, egg and buttermilk together and stir into the dry ingredients until it forms a ball.

Place the dough on a floured surface. Knead lightly a few times and roll out until it's about 1/2 inch (1.2 cm) thick. Cut into rounds with a floured cutter. Place on a greased cookie sheet and bake about 18-20 minutes, until the tops are lightly browned.

CHAPTER THREE

Garlic — The Winter Flavor Staple

arlic is as good as ten mothers," is one of the many aphorisms written about garlic. Many claims are made for garlic in the health and herbal worlds, but as a cook I think the most important claim is the wonderful, intense flavor it adds to our winter cooking. Last summer's harvest hanging in net onion bags, waiting to be cooked, is good insurance against the dull of days of winter.

There are racks of various garlic-based supplements in health food stores. Some call it Russian penicillin and it does have antibacterial qualities, but putting it in your food instead of popping garlic pills is a lot more pleasurable and you get the beneficial effects as well.

Harvested in late July, the garlic is cured in the sun for a few days and then hung up in a dry cool place. Ancient Greeks, Romans and Egyptians used garlic for food and medicine and the "stinking rose" has been associated with herb gardens and cooking for centuries. If you are put off by garlic's reputation, a few cooking tips will help. Garlic cooked until it is very dark brown will become acrid and too pungent. Finely chopped garlic, gently sautéed over low heat until it is a pale gold color, will give dishes a flavor boost. Whole cloves sautéed, boiled or baked are sweet and gentle on the palate. Raw garlic (as in aioli sauce) is the most potent. I no longer worry about dreaded garlic breath. The solution is to feed garlic to yourself and your nearest and dearest and be healthy and happy.

Baked Garlic

Serve these garlic bulbs with a basket of hot French bread. Your dinner guests can squeeze the garlic onto hot bread. With a glass of stout red wine, this makes a wonderful appetizer.

garlic bulbs, one per person

olive oil

Preheat oven to 375°F (190°C). Leaving the garlic bulbs whole, snip away the untidy bits. Rub each bulb with olive oil. Place in a small baking dish and bake uncovered about 1 1/2 hours. The interior of the garlic will be smooth and creamy.

Garlic Dip

Use this as a dip for cocktail meatballs, chicken shish kebabs, raw vegetables or to cool off a curry. Makes 1 cup (250 mL).

1 cup (250 mL) low-fat or regular yogurt

2 cloves garlic, peeled and very finely minced

2 Tbsp. (30 mL) frozen snipped chives

4 Tbsp. (60 mL) freshly chopped parsley or cilantro

freshly ground pepper, to taste

Mix all ingredients together, cover and refrigerate until ready to use.

Stuffed Mushrooms with Garlic

I cannot resist taking home extra-large mushrooms from the market, and then stuffing them with savory cheese, parsley and garlic. Use them as a vegetable side dish, as a first course or to surround a roast. Serves 4.

6-8 perfect large mushrooms

2-4 Tbsp. (25-60 mL) olive or other vegetable oil

2 cloves garlic, peeled and finely chopped

1 shallot, peeled and finely chopped

1/2 cup (125 mL) fresh breadcrumbs

1/2 cup (125 mL) chopped parsley

1/2 cup (125 mL) grated Parmesan cheese

freshly ground pepper

chopped parsley, as garnish

Preheat the oven to 350°F (180°C). Gently wiggle the stems loose from the mushroom caps. Set aside. With a small sharp knife, hollow out more room in the mushroom. Heat 1 Tbsp. (15 mL) of the oil in a nonstick pan, and cook the mushroom caps top side down on medium heat for 4-5 minutes. Remove from frying pan and set them aside.

Add the rest of the oil to the pan and sauté the garlic and shallot until soft and just turning golden. Chop the mushroom stems and add to the shallot and garlic. Cook for a few minutes. Add the breadcrumbs, parsley, Parmesan and pepper. Mix well and remove from heat. Mixture will be moist and crumbly.

Place the mushrooms in a flat baking dish and stuff each one with the crumb mixture. Bake for 30 minutes. Spoon the mushroom juices in the bottom of the dish over the baked mushrooms just before serving. Sprinkle chopped parsley over the tops for decoration.

Aioli Sauce

Aioli is usually made at the farm in late July when the first garlic is harvested, but it is such amazing stuff, it should be made in winter. It is often called the butter of Provence and villages have aioli parties to celebrate the garlic harvest. Vegetables, fresh cod, shrimp, and fresh bread are dipped into this powerful sauce. I have served it on pasta, toasted French bread, barbecued meats and any vegetable, raw or cooked. Originally made with a mortar and pestle, it is now simple to make in a food processor. It has such flavor, it truly is a hymn to garlic. Makes about 2 cups (500 mL).

8-12 cloves garlic, peeled

2 large egg yolks, at room temperature

freshly ground pepper and a dash of salt

juice of 1 lemon

1 tsp. (5 mL) Dijon mustard

1 1/2 cups (375 mL) olive oil

Purée the garlic in the food processor. Whisk the egg yolks in a small bowl until light and smooth. Add to garlic in processor. Add salt and pepper, lemon juice and mustard to garlic and eggs. Process until smooth. Slowly add oil while the machine is running. Process until the sauce is thick, yellow, shiny and firm. Refrigerate until ready to use.

For a basil-flavored variation, add 1 cup (250 mL) packed basil leaves to the garlic in the processor. (You can use some of your basil frozen in oil for this.)

Serve the aioli in a bowl on a large platter. Surround it with vegetables, cooked fish, shrimp and other favorite foods and have an aioli party in December.

Garlic Vinaigrette

A robust salad dressing, this vinaigrette will keep in the refrigerator for a week. Besides using it on salads, brush it on roast chicken or use it as a marinade. Makes 1 cup (250 mL).

1-3 cloves garlic, peeled

3/4 cup (175 mL) olive oil or other vegetable oil

1/4 cup (50 mL) herb or garlic vinegar (red or white)

freshly ground pepper

pinch of white sugar

Press garlic cloves with the flat side of a large chopping knife to mash them. The amount you use depends on your bravery. Whisk all ingredients together in a bowl until emulsified. Refrigerate in a jar with a good cap. Serve at room temperature. Shake well before using.

Garlic Butter

An excellent flavoring agent, garlic butter can be brushed on fish, chicken, vegetables and, of course, crusty bread. It can be frozen in a roll in aluminum foil or in little crocks, which make good gifts for garlic lovers. Makes 2 1/2 cups (625 mL).

4-6 cloves garlic, peeled and dropped into boiling water for two minutes

1 lb. (500 g) butter or margarine

freshly ground pepper

1/2 cup (125 mL) chopped parsley (optional)

1 Tbsp. (15 mL) horseradish sauce

1 Tbsp. (15 mL) Dijon mustard

Process garlic cloves in the food processor. Add butter or margarine in chunks and process until soft and creamy. Add remaining ingredients and blend well. Place the butter on a piece of foil and form it into a roll. Freeze and cut off pieces as needed.

Garlic Mashed Potatoes

In this dish, garlic adds new life to an old favorite. The powerful flavor of the garlic adds a richness to the bland smoothness of mashed potatoes. If there are any leftovers you can form the potatoes into small cakes and sauté them. Serves 4.

4-6 cups (1-1.5 L) mashed potatoes

4 cloves garlic, peeled and left whole

1/2 cup (125 mL) chopped parsley (optional)

3 Tbsp. (45 mL) butter or margarine (optional)

Prepare your usual mashed potatoes. Set aside and keep warm. Place garlic in a saucepan of boiling water and simmer for five minutes, until soft. Remove from water and in a small bowl mash garlic with a fork until it is creamy. Add a little of the garlic water to make the purée a little thinner. Add the garlic to the mashed potatoes and whip well with a masher.

If desired, add chopped parsley, mix well, dot with butter or margarine and put under the broiler for a minute or so, until it is brown and bubbly.

Garlic Cooked in Balsamic Vinegar

Balsamic vinegar, which is found in specialty stores, has been stored in wooden barrels and aged like good sherry. It adds a rich, intense flavor to vegetables, meats and sauces. The garlic can be cooked on top of the stove in a frying pan or baked covered in the oven. Use it to top a pizza or as part of an antipasto platter. Makes 2 cups (500 mL).

2 cups (500 mL) garlic cloves, peeled and left whole

4 Tbsp. (60 mL) olive oil

1/2 cup (125 mL) balsamic vinegar

Put garlic, oil and vinegar in a heavy-bottomed frying pan. Bring to a boil and let simmer for 25-30 minutes. The vinegar and oil will thicken and the garlic will be soft and sweet tasting.

To make in the oven, place all ingredients in a covered casserole in a 350°F (180°C) oven. Cook 30 to 40 minutes.

Garlic Vinegar

Add crushed cloves of garlic to homemade tarragon vinegar for a savory marinade. It's excellent for pot roasts or venison and a great addition to dressings for coleslaw. Makes 1 quart (1 L).

10 cloves garlic, peeled and slightly crushed with the flat side of a chopping knife

4-8 black peppercorns

shreds of lemon rind

4 cups (1 L) tarragon vinegar or plain red wine vinegar

Place garlic cloves, peppercorns and lemon rind in sterilized bottles. Heat the vinegar in a saucepan until it is just boiling. Pour the vinegar into the bottles. Cap tightly and let steep in a cool dark cupboard for a few weeks.

Bean and Garlic Purée with Sage and Winter Savory

This is a new twist on reliable old baked beans. Serve it with grilled sausages, hamburgers, eggs, chops, or on toast or with a salad for a vegetarian lunch. Cheap, healthy, high-fibre food can taste wonderful — the proof is in this flavorful recipe. Serves 6-8.

1 lb. (500 g) small navy beans, soaked overnight

3/4 cup (175 mL) olive oil

1 cup (250 mL) beef stock, or lovage stock, and enough water to cover the beans

2 bay leaves

4 fresh or frozen sage leaves, or 1 tsp. (5 mL) dried

6 cloves garlic, peeled

freshly ground pepper and salt, if desired

Place beans in an ovenproof ceramic or enameled pot with a good lid. Add remaining ingredients and mix well. Cover and bake three or four hours, until all the liquid is absorbed and the beans are soft.

Remove bay, sage, and winter savory leaves. Place beans in the food processor and purée until smooth. Add extra olive oil if it is too thick. Serve warm or at room temperature.

Brown Rice Cooked with Bay and Garlic

Country cooking has always relied on members of the onion family. If food sources are limited, flavors that enliven the staples become extra valuable to the kitchen repertoire. Try this garlicky version of that old standby, brown rice. Serves 4.

6 cloves garlic, peeled and left whole

2 Tbsp. (30 mL) olive oil

1 cup (250 mL) raw brown rice

2 bay leaves

2 1/2 cups (625 mL) chicken stock

1 cup (250 mL) cooked shrimp or chicken (optional)

chopped parsley or cilantro, as garnish

Sauté the garlic cloves in the olive oil for 4-5 minutes. Do not burn or overbrown. Stir in the rice and cook for 3-4 minutes. Put rice, garlic, bay leaves and chicken stock in a heavy-bottomed saucepan. Bring to a boil, then reduce to simmer. Cover and cook for about 45 minutes.

If desired, cooked shrimp or chicken may be stirred into the rice at the end. Sprinkle with chopped parsley or cilantro and serve immediately.

Braised Garlic

Use this garlic dish as a vegetable side dish — delicious with roast pork or roast chicken. Serves 4.

4 whole bulbs garlic, separated and peeled

6-8 Tbsp. (90-120 mL) butter, margarine or oil

1/2 cup (125 mL) finely chopped green onions

freshly ground pepper

Simmer the garlic cloves in boiling water for 12-15 minutes, until tender. Drain cloves and sauté gently in butter until just golden brown. Stir in the chopped green onions. Put in a warmed serving dish. Season with pepper and serve.

Tapenade

This spicy, black, Provençal olive paste is a winter standby. Spread it on crackers, use it as a veggie dip, stuff eggs and tomatoes with it or put it on pasta. You may use highly flavored and salty Greek and Italian olives or the milder California variety. The following recipe was developed for a garlic and basil cooking class. Omit the basil if you wish or substitute a dollop of basil pesto. Makes 1 cup (250 mL).

1 cup (250 mL) pitted black olives

3 cloves garlic, peeled

1 2-oz (50-g) can anchovies, drained and rinsed

1/4 cup (50 mL) chopped fresh or frozen basil

1/2 cup (125 mL) olive oil

Place all ingredients, except for the oil, in the food processor. Process until smooth, then slowly add the oil as the machine is running. Put the tapenade in a bowl and serve with crisp toast, melba rounds or on pasta. Store in the refrigerator in a sterilized jar with a tight lid. Tapenade will keep for a month in the refrigerator.

CHAPTER FOUR

Hearty Herbed Meat and Poultry

---

*W*hen I envision a winter supper I think of the dark and rainy outside world and then I visualize a comforting, cozy interior, such as the safe, warm kitchen of my childhood with a large silver and black McClary stove with nickel-plated curves. On the stove a stew full of beef and carrots and onions bubbles away.

Winter food should be comforting, robust and flavorful. I like making my kitchen and dinner time a special place and time so it becomes a refuge full of tantalizing smells. It re-creates the secure pleasures of my childhood and makes the world seem serene and happy.

Meat dishes with rich flavors that have developed from simmering on the stove seem to go well with cold weather. They fill the kitchen with good smells and the comforting knowledge that you can pursue another activity guilt-free, for dinner is already prepared.

Bay leaves, sage, rosemary, thyme and winter savory — grown on a sunny window sill or dried and frozen — are my favorite herbs for meat dishes. They have strong opinionated flavors that survive long simmering and cut the fatty taste of meat.

Lazy Cook's Unrolled Cabbage Rolls

Why fuss with cabbage rolls when this simple cabbage dish tastes so good? You can substitute pork or veal for the ground beef; sometimes I add leftover ham. Serves 4.

2-4 Tbsp. (30-60 mL) vegetable oil

1 lb. (500 g) ground beef

1 medium onion, finely chopped

2-4 cloves garlic, peeled and finely chopped

6-8 mushrooms, chopped

freshly ground pepper

1 Tbsp. (15 mL) finely chopped rosemary

1 bay leaf

1 1/2 cups (375 mL) cooked rice

1 medium to large green cabbage

1 1/2-2 cups (375-500 mL) beef stock

1/2 cup (125 mL) fresh breadcrumbs

2 cup (500 mL) grated sharp Cheddar cheese

Heat the oil in a large frying pan and sauté the beef, onion, garlic and mushrooms with the pepper, rosemary and bay leaf. Cook for about five minutes, until the meat is no longer red. Remove the bay leaf. Stir the cooked rice into the mixture and set aside.

Bring a large pot of water to a boil. Separate the leaves from the cabbage and drop them into the water. Cook two or three minutes until softened. Drain well and set aside.

Grease a large, ovenproof casserole. Line the bottom with a layer of the wilted cabbage leaves. Cover with a layer of the meat and rice mixture, and add another layer of cabbage. Continue until all the ingredients are used. Gently pour the beef stock over the layers. Mix breadcrumbs and cheese together and sprinkle over the top. Bake in a 350°F (180°C) oven for one hour. Serve hot with crusty bread, and pickles and chutney.

Barbecued and Butterflied Leg of Lamb with Rosemary and Thyme

Cooking on a barbecue does not have to be restricted to the summer months. This lamb can also be cooked on an electric indoor grill, or under the broiler in your oven, using the same directions. You might need a smaller leg of lamb or have to cut one in two smaller pieces. As we raise lamb at Ravenhill, I am always looking for wonderful ways of cooking it. This version, based on Edena Sheldon's recipe in Canada Cooks, Barbecue *is the best lamb barbecue I have cooked or eaten. I serve it on a big wooden chopping board with grilled vegetables, baked potatoes and an assortment of mustards, horseradish and herbed jellies. It has become a celebration dinner for visiting friends and relatives. Serves 6-10.*

1 leg of lamb, about 6-8 lbs. (3-4 kg), boned and butterflied

1/2 cup (125 mL) olive oil

6 cloves garlic, peeled and crushed

2 Tbsp. (30 mL) fresh or frozen chopped thyme or
  2 tsp. (10 mL) dried

2 Tbsp. (30 mL) fresh or frozen chopped rosemary or
  2 tsp. (10 mL) dried

1/2 cup (125mL) dry red wine

freshly ground pepper

sprigs of rosemary and thyme, as garnish

Press the boned lamb out flat in a large flat dish. Brush with olive oil. Sprinkle with garlic, herbs and wine. Marinate overnight, turning regularly.

To barbecue, heat coals for 45 minutes, or for 5 minutes if using a gas barbecue. Oil grill. Place grill 4-6 inches (10-15 cm) above the coals. Place lamb on grill and sear each side 10 minutes.

Brush with marinade. Continue to grill lamb, turning and basting, for 35-45 minutes total time for medium-rare. Cook 15 minutes more for medium. Thicker parts of the lamb will be pink and thin parts will be well done, so you can please everybody. Sprinkle with freshly ground pepper to taste. Let it rest on a warm platter before carving. Decorate with sprigs of rosemary and thyme.

Rack of Lamb with Marmalade

I found this outstanding way to do a rack of lamb in a Madame Benoit lamb cookbook now sadly out of print. Rice and crisply cooked zucchini are good partners for this lamb dish. Serves 2-4.

1 3- to 4-lb. (1.5- to 2-kg) rack of lamb

1/2 cup (125 mL) Japanese soya sauce

1/4 cup (50 mL) Seville orange marmalade

1 Tbsp. (15 mL) grated fresh ginger

juice of 1 lemon

water or a dash of vermouth

Preheat oven to 400°F (200°C). Put lamb in a roasting pan and roast uncovered for 30 minutes. Mix soya sauce, marmalade, ginger and lemon juice and pour over the rack. Roast for 20-25 minutes more. It will be pink inside; cook 15-20 minutes longer if you like your lamb well done. Add some water or vermouth to the pan juices. Stir until heated and serve with the lamb.

Clay Cooker Veal with Winter Vegetables

*Easy to assemble, this dish can contain whatever winter vegetables
are available. Supermarkets always have a good supply of turnips,
parsnips, carrots and onions. I also like to add fennel and mushrooms.
Get a narrow roll of veal, which will fit better in the clay baker and
cook quicker. A rolled, boned roast of pork, which is cheaper than
veal, is also very good. If you do not have a clay baker, use a heavy
pot with a good lid, or a pottery casserole. Serves 6-8.*

3- to 4-lb. (1.5- to 2-kg) veal roast, boned and rolled

freshly ground pepper

2 Tbsp. (30 mL) finely chopped rosemary

1/4 cup (50 mL) all-purpose flour

3 Tbsp. (45 mL) olive oil

1 cup (250 mL) red wine

1 cup (250 mL) beef stock

2 bay leaves

6 small potatoes, peeled

4 carrots, sliced in rounds

10 mushrooms, sliced

6 shallots, peeled and left whole

4 cloves garlic, peeled and left whole

1 small turnip, peeled and cubed

2-4 parsnips, peeled and cut into rounds

1 small fennel bulb, diced

3 Tbsp. (45 mL) chopped parsley

rosemary sprigs

If using a clay baker, soak both top and bottom in water for 15 minutes. Mix pepper, rosemary and flour together on a plate. Roll the veal roast in the flour mixture.

In a large heavy frying pan, heat the olive oil and brown the veal on all sides. Place the veal in the bottom of the clay baker. Add all the other ingredients except for the chopped parsley and rosemary sprigs. Cover and cook for 1 1/2 hours in a 400°F (200°C) oven. Do not preheat. Test for doneness. The vegetables should be very tender and the veal faintly pink. Depending on the thickness of the meat, it might take another 15 to 30 minutes.

Slice meat very thinly and arrange on a warmed platter. Surround meat with the cooked vegetables. Sprinkle with chopped parsley and rosemary sprigs. Skim any excess fat off the pan juices and serve juices in a gravy jug with the veal.

Winter Savory Pork and Veal Meatballs

Winter savory has a clean piny taste that is a nice addition to pork and veal dishes. You can vary the meats in this dish, using beef or all pork. Serves 4-6.

1 lb. (500 g) ground pork

1 lb. (500 g) ground veal

dash of soya sauce

2 Tbsp. (30 mL) finely chopped winter savory

2 Tbsp. (30 mL) finely chopped fresh parsley

1 cup (250 mL) fresh breadcrumbs

2 shallots, finely chopped

Preheat oven to 450°F (230°C). Mix all ingredients in a large bowl. Form into meatballs and either sauté them in a large frying pan or cook in the oven on a cookie sheet for 10-12 minutes. You can make these meatballs either cocktail-sized or dinner-sized.

Beef Stew with Onion, Mushrooms and Orange Rind

Using orange rind in meat dishes is very common in the South of France and adds a fillip to the taste. Sometimes I add some tiny frozen peas at the end. This dish is a complete meal in a pot, with a crusty peasant loaf to help mop up the gravy. Serves 4-6.

2 lbs. (1 kg) stewing beef, cut into cubes

4 Tbsp. (60 mL) flour, enough to dredge the meat

freshly ground pepper

dash of cayenne pepper

4 Tbsp. (60 mL) vegetable oil

4 medium onions (red or yellow), thinly sliced

4-6 cloves garlic, peeled and minced

1 lb. (500 g) mushrooms, sliced

3-4 long thin strips orange rind

6 carrots, peeled and sliced in rounds

1 cup (250 mL) beef stock, fresh or canned

1 cup (250 mL) dry red wine

3 bay leaves (preferably fresh, as they have the most fragrance)

Preheat oven to 350°F (175°C). Toss beef cubes in a bag with flour, pepper and cayenne until the beef cubes are well floured. Heat oil in a large frying pan and brown the cubes of meat on all sides. Remove meat to an ovenproof baking dish or a Dutch oven.

Sauté the onions, garlic and mushrooms for a few minutes in the frying pan and then add to the meat.

Add orange rind and sliced carrots to the frying pan. Pour the beef stock and red wine over the carrots and bring to a boil. Scrape up the browned bits with a spoon. Pour carrots, wine and stock over meat and vegetables. Add bay leaves and a little more ground pepper. Cover and bake for 1 1/2 hours. Cook a little longer if needed, adding extra liquid if necessary. Remove bay leaves before serving.

Pork Tenderloin and Leek Sauté with Fresh Ginger

Leeks are readily available in supermarkets all year round, and on the west coast, they stand upright in our winter garden like kitchen soldiers waiting to be called for duty. Pork tenderloin, though expensive, is waste free, quick to cook, and delicious. Serve on a bed of noodles, with some herb jelly on the side. Serves 4.

1 1/2 lbs. (750 g) pork tenderloin

3 Tbsp. (45 mL) soya sauce

4 Tbsp. (60 mL) vegetable oil

4 medium leeks, chopped in rounds and washed carefully

2 cloves garlic, peeled and finely chopped

1/4 cup (50 mL) fresh ginger, peeled and sliced very thinly

freshly ground pepper

1/2 cup (125 mL) chicken stock

splash of dry vermouth

1/4 cup (50 mL) chopped parsley

Slice the pork tenderloin in very thin rounds. Place in a bowl and sprinkle with soya sauce. Set aside.

Heat vegetable oil in a large frying pan. When oil is hot, add pork. Keeping the heat fairly high, stir and turn the pork as it changes color, for about 3-4 minutes. Add leeks, garlic, ginger and pepper. Stir and cook for 5 minutes. Add chicken stock and vermouth. Cook for 4-5 minutes. The sauce should reduce; if it disappears, add a little water or more vermouth.

Serve on a warmed platter over hot cooked noodles. Sprinkle with chopped parsley before serving.

Herbed Shepherd's Pie

Food snobs may sneer at Shepherd's Pie, but most people secretly love this comforting food. As James Barber says, everyone likes it — from the young to the toothless. My version is like my mother's but it is herbed and garlicked, which increases its flavor. I often serve cooked red cabbage with this and some good sharp pickles, and I confess I love catsup with Shepherd's Pie. Serves 4-6.

6 medium potatoes, peeled and quartered

3 Tbsp. (45 mL) butter or margarine

3 Tbsp. (45 mL) parsley

milk to moisten

2 large onions, finely chopped

4-6 cloves garlic, peeled and finely chopped

3 Tbsp. (45 mL) vegetable oil

2 lbs. (1 kg) ground beef, or ground-up leftover pork or lamb

2 tsp. (10 mL) finely chopped rosemary

1 tsp. (5 mL) finely chopped winter savory

2 Tbsp. (30 mL) frozen chopped chives or chopped green onions

2 Tbsp. (30 mL) chopped parsley

dash of soya sauce

1/2 cup (125 mL) beef stock

dash of red wine

freshly ground pepper

2 Tbsp. (30 mL) butter or margarine

dusting of paprika

Cook potatoes in boiling water until tender. Drain and mash them with butter, parsley and enough milk to make them creamy. Set aside. Preheat oven to 350°F (175°C).

In a large frying pan, sauté the onions and the garlic in oil for 2-3 minutes. Stir in the ground meat and cook until the meat changes color, 4 to 5 minutes. Stir in the herbs, soya sauce, beef stock, a dash of wine and the pepper.

Place the meat mixture in an ovenproof casserole dish and spoon the mashed potatoes over the top. Dot with butter or margarine and dust with paprika. Bake for 30 minutes, until the crust is brown and the meat is bubbling underneath. If necessary, flick on the broiler for a few minutes to brown the top.

Turkey Burgers

Ground turkey is a most versatile meat. It has less fat and cholesterol than other meats and can be substituted for them in all your ground meat recipes. Turkey burgers full of chopped shallots and chives make a delicious, quick supper. Serve them on pieces of crusty bread with lettuce, tomatoes, onions and lots of condiments. Serves 4.

1 1/2 lbs. (750 g) ground turkey

4 shallots, peeled and finely chopped

1 beaten egg

1 Tbsp. (15 mL) tamari soya sauce

3 Tbsp. (45 mL) frozen chopped chives or chopped green onions

freshly ground pepper

1 Tbsp. (15 mL) horseradish sauce

Mix all ingredients together in a bowl and form into eight small to medium patties. Cook for about 4-5 minutes on each side. This turkey burger mix can be used to make meatballs or a meat loaf. Bake the loaf for 1 hour in a 350°F (180°C) oven or bake individual servings in muffin tins for 20-25 minutes.

Lemon Chicken

Bowls of lemons and oranges add bright globes of color to the winter kitchen. In Provence cooks save and dry orange and lemon peel to use in winter dishes and cordials. For this tart, tangy dish, you can use any parts of the chicken, but I often use legs and thighs. Serves 4.

3/4 cup (175 mL) fresh lemon juice

4 Tbsp. (60 mL) chopped fresh lemon thyme or 2 tsp. (10 mL) dried

3 Tbsp. (45 mL) vegetable oil

1/4 cup (50 mL) dry vermouth

freshly ground pepper

8 chicken legs with thighs attached

4 Tbsp. (60 mL) butter or margarine

2 lemons, sliced

lemon thyme sprigs, as garnish

Mix lemon juice, lemon thyme, oil, vermouth and pepper together in a bowl. Place chicken pieces in a flat ceramic baking dish and pour marinade over them. Marinate overnight, or for at least four hours. Stir and turn chicken pieces occasionally.

Remove chicken from marinade and pat dry with paper towel. Heat butter or margarine in a large heavy frying pan and brown chicken, about 8-10 minutes on each side. Put chicken on a platter and keep warm.

Add marinade to the frying pan, bring to a boil and reduce to about 1/2 cup (125 mL). Return chicken to the frying pan and spoon the sauce over it. Place on the platter, and drizzle remaining sauce over the chicken. Decorate with thin slices of lemon and sprigs of fresh lemon thyme.

Stuffed Chicken Breasts with Cilantro Pesto

The exotic smell and taste of cilantro raises this chicken dish out of the humdrum. Served with rice, a salad and a spicy chutney, it's a good dish for a gray day. Serves 4.

Cilantro Pesto (page 15)

2 whole chicken breasts with the skin on, cut in half

2 Tbsp. (30 mL) olive oil

cilantro sprigs, as garnish

Have ready one recipe of Cilantro Pesto. Preheat oven to 375°F (190°C).

With your fingers, loosen the skin of the chicken breasts, being careful to leave it attached around the edges. Spoon the cilantro pesto under the skin, so the whole breast area is covered with pesto. Lay chicken pieces in a baking dish, side by side, skin side up. Brush the tops with olive oil.

Bake 35-40 minutes, until the chicken is golden brown. Serve on a bed of rice and drizzle some of the drippings and pesto from the pan over the chicken and rice. Decorate with sprigs of cilantro.

Roast Chicken Stuffed with Goat Cheese and Garlic

Serve this most impressive roast chicken dish for company. The skin is golden and puffy and the goat cheese and garlic flavor is intense and rich. If desired, substitute Cornish game hens for chicken. Rosemary jelly, pan-roasted potatoes with rosemary and puréed squash complete the meal. Serves 4-6.

1 large roasting chicken

8 oz. (250 g) mild goat cheese or cream cheese

4 cloves garlic, finely chopped

freshly ground pepper

4-6 Tbsp. (60-90 mL) olive oil

dash of vermouth

Preheat oven to 400°F (200°C). Rinse the chicken under cold water and pat dry with paper towels. In a bowl, mash the cheese, garlic and pepper into a smooth paste. Loosen the skin of the chicken breasts with your fingers and push the cheese mixture under the skin. Rub the skin of the chicken with olive oil, massaging the oil into the skin. This makes it crispy.

Place the chicken in a roasting pan. Splash some vermouth over it. Roast the chicken for about 1 hour and 15 minutes, basting every 15 minutes with pan drippings or some extra olive oil. It should be crisp and brown. Place the chicken on a warmed platter. Skim the fat off the pan juices and serve the juices as a sauce.

CHAPTER FIVE

Winter Soups

Soup is one of the most important winter pleasures. It is comforting, nourishing, flavorful and amazingly inexpensive to make. The cook only needs some cooked, puréed vegetables, some stock and a sprinkling of herbs for the beginning of a perfect meal — that other staple, bread, will round it off nicely. With a well-stocked cupboard and freezer, the cook can make soup for dinner in half an hour.

Keeping a supply of stock on hand is important for soup makers. Canned or frozen, stock is the base from which all soups grow. I often throw the remains of a roast chicken in a pot with some herbs, an onion and water and in half an hour there is some stock to tuck in the freezer. Vegetable stock can be made with potatoes and potato peelings. In September I make lovage stock (see page 4). With its strong celery flavor, it is an excellent base for soup. Herbs such as lovage, parsley, chives, tarragon and bay leaves do wonders to improve the flavor of stocks, and you will need less salt or no salt at all.

In my pantry cupboard I keep lentils, split peas, dried beans, chick peas, various types of noodles, rice and canned tomatoes. In November and December I prowl through our winter garden looking for soup ingredients. I can usually find leeks, vegetable fennel, Russian kale, carrots, beets, celeriac, Swiss chard and arugula. Happily, nearly all these vegetables are available in markets.

Two bay trees sit on my kitchen window sill all winter. A fresh bay leaf in the soup will perfume your kitchen. Sprinkle some fresh or frozen chopped herb on top of the soup when serving, for a finished, decorative touch, a splash of green color and an added flick to your taste buds.

Soup and bread dinners are nourishing and low in calories, but they are tasty enough to serve to company. Sprinkling extras such as cheese, homemade croutons, chopped herbs, and sour cream or yogurt on top of the soup makes it more attractive and adds extra nutrition. The final word on soup comes from an old Spanish proverb, which holds that "of soup and love, the first is best."

Winter Tomato Soup

Here is an easy, delicious soup you can make in winter out of your stash of frozen tomatoes. Serves 4.

6-8 frozen tomatoes

2-3 cloves garlic, peeled and finely chopped

1/4 cup (50 mL) snipped frozen herbs (dill, tarragon or chives)

freshly ground pepper

2 cups (500 mL) chicken, beef or vegetable stock

dash of hot pepper sauce, if desired

yogurt, as garnish

chopped parsley, as garnish

Run the tomatoes under warm water to remove the skins. Thaw. Place in a food processor with the garlic, herbs and pepper. Process for a few seconds.

Combine tomato mixture and stock in a saucepan. Heat to boiling and simmer for five minutes. Add a dash of hot pepper sauce, to spice the soup up, if desired. Serve with a dollop of yogurt and some chopped parsley.

Carrot Soup with Lemon Thyme and Lemon

A pot of lemon thyme on your window sill or a supply of dried thyme will give this soup its herbal flavor. Carrots and citrus flavors go well together. This is a bright elegant soup to begin a dinner party. Serves 4.

4 cups (1 L) peeled carrots, sliced in rounds

2 bay leaves

3 leeks, washed and sliced in rounds

3 Tbsp. (45 mL) fresh lemon juice

freshly ground pepper

4 Tbsp. (60 mL) freshly chopped lemon thyme or 2 Tbsp. (30 mL) dried thyme

5 cups (1.25 L) chicken stock

a few lemon thyme sprigs, for decoration

1 lemon, thinly sliced

Cook the peeled, sliced carrots until tender in a large saucepan with a small amount of water and the two bay leaves. Add leeks, lemon juice, pepper, lemon thyme and chicken stock to the carrots and carrot water. Simmer about 20 minutes.

Remove the bay leaves. Purée the vegetables in a processor. Heat the soup through. To serve, place a sprig of lemon thyme and a very thin slice of lemon on the top of each serving.

Christmas Eve Borscht

Beets make a rich colorful soup for winter. They are available in markets all winter and can be frozen or canned. Borscht recipes vary a great deal. Some are full of cabbage and chopped beets and some are more aristocratic and are like a beet consommé — all the good solid ingredients are thrown out and you sip the beet-colored stock. I prefer the peasant soup, full of vegetables and with a dollop of sour cream or yogurt on top. Borscht is a delicious soup to serve on Christmas Eve with coarse whole-wheat bread. It is a good contrast to the feasting on Christmas day. Serves 6.

8 cups (2 L) beef stock

4 cups (1 L) diced cooked beets

2 potatoes, peeled and thinly sliced

2 medium onions, peeled and finely chopped

2 cups (500 mL) finely chopped cabbage

2 bay leaves

freshly ground pepper

1/2 lb. (250 g) lean stewing beef (optional)

1/4 cup (50 mL) fresh lemon juice

pinch of sugar

sour cream or yogurt, as garnish

finely chopped green onion, as garnish

In a large saucepan, bring the beef stock to a boil. Add the beets, potatoes, onions, cabbage, bay leaves and pepper. If you want to add meat, cut stewing beef into small cubes and add at this point. Cook for about 25 minutes.

You can purée the soup in a food processor or stir it well and leave it chunky (do not purée the soup if you added meat). Add lemon juice and a pinch of sugar to give the soup a mild sweet-sour flavor. Serve with a spoonful of sour cream or yogurt on top and a bowl of finely chopped green onions on the side.

Pumpkin Soup with Homemade Croutons

Pumpkins and squash decorate my kitchen from harvest time through the winter, until I have made the last one into soup, pie, or a decorative container for chili. The brilliant glow of orange on a gray winter day gladdens the cook's heart. This pumpkin soup is smooth, creamy and delicate and is perked up with chopped herbs, croutons and cheese. Serves 6.

4 cups (1 L) cooked pumpkin purée (or substitute squash)

4 cups (1 L) light cream or milk

1 tsp. (5 mL) sugar

dash of salt

freshly ground pepper

sprinkle of nutmeg

2 cups (500 mL) Homemade Croutons (recipe follows)

1/2 cup (125 mL) chopped herbs (parsley, chives or green onions)

1/2 cup (125 mL) grated Swiss or Parmesan cheese

You can use canned or frozen pumpkin in this recipe. If you are cooking your pumpkin from scratch, cut it in half or in quarters. Scoop out the seeds and stringy parts. Wrap in aluminum foil and place on a baking pan. Bake at 400°F (200°C) for about one hour, until soft. Scoop the cooked pumpkin out of the shell and purée in a food processor.

To make the soup, place puréed pumpkin in a large saucepan. Whisk in the cream or milk, sugar, salt, pepper and nutmeg. Simmer slowly for 15 minutes. Soup should be just bubbling. Pour soup into warmed bowls and sprinkle with croutons, chopped herbs and grated cheese.

Homemade Croutons

4-6 slices bread, cubed

4 Tbsp. (60 mL) olive oil

1 clove garlic, peeled and chopped (optional)

Sauté cubed bread in the olive oil. Some peeled and chopped garlic may be added for flavor. Stir well until croutons are crisp and brown. Place croutons on paper toweling to soak up any excess oil.

Vichysoisse

Traditionally made with leeks, I have often substituted onions and shallots in vichysoisse. Instead of the usual cream, I have found milk quite satisfactory. The soup still has a creamy texture but has less fat. Serves 6-8.

2 cups (500 mL) washed and finely chopped leeks

4 Tbsp. (60 mL) butter or margarine

8 cups (2 L) potatoes, peeled and sliced

6 cups (1.5 L) chicken stock

4 cups (1 L) 2 percent milk, or cream

freshly ground pepper

dash of nutmeg

chopped chives, parsley or green onions, as garnish

In a large saucepan, sauté the washed, chopped leeks in the butter or margarine until soft (about 5 minutes).

Add potatoes and chicken stock to the leeks and simmer for 20 minutes, until potatoes are soft. Purée the soup in batches in the food processor. Return it to the saucepan and add the milk, pepper and nutmeg. Sprinkle soup with chopped herbs and serve hot in winter or cold in summer.

Chick Pea and Orzo Soup with Rosemary and Garlic

I make this in my slow cooker, but a heavy-bottomed saucepan will do. You can use canned chick peas or prepare dried ones. Soak dried chick peas overnight and then simmer them with a bay leaf and a sprig of lemon thyme for an hour, or until tender. Freeze the extra chick peas or store in the refrigerator to make humus or to put in salads. Serves 6.

3 cloves garlic, finely chopped

1 large onion, finely chopped

2 tsp. (10 mL) finely chopped fresh rosemary or 1 tsp. (5 mL) dried

1/4 cup (50 mL) olive oil or vegetable oil

2 cups (500 mL) canned tomatoes or your own frozen tomatoes

1 20-oz. (570-mL) can chick peas or 2 cups (500 mL) prepared chick peas

4 cups (1 L) beef stock

2/3 cup (150 mL) orzo pasta

salt, to taste

freshly ground pepper

1/2 cup (125 mL) chopped parsley

freshly grated Parmesan cheese

In a large saucepan, sauté the garlic, onion and rosemary in oil until the onion is soft, about five minutes. Add tomatoes and chick peas. Cook for 15 minutes. Add beef stock, orzo and salt and pepper. Heat thoroughly and let simmer for twenty minutes before serving, or put in a slow cooker on low for the day and go for a hike. Serve the soup with bowls of chopped parsley and Parmesan cheese.

Sorrel and Lentil Soup

Sorrel is impossible to buy in markets, so in order to have this lemony spinachlike herb you need to grow it in your garden or in a pot on your deck. I always freeze some sorrel in the fall so it is already cooked and puréed. You just need to slip it into a soup recipe or into a sauce. Spinach and a squirt of lemon juice could be substituted for sorrel in this recipe. Serves 4-6.

1 cup (250 mL) dried green lentils

1 large onion, finely chopped

4 1/2 cups (1.125 L) chicken stock

2 bay leaves

sprig of lemon thyme

2 cups (500 mL) sorrel purée (recipe page 3)

1 cup (250 mL) low-fat yogurt

freshly ground pepper

chopped fresh parsley

Wash the lentils. Place in a saucepan with the onion, chicken stock, bay leaves and lemon thyme. Bring to a boil and simmer covered for an hour or longer, until lentils are soft. If the soup is very thick, add some extra chicken stock or water.

Remove the bay leaf and the thyme sprig and purée in a food processor. Stir in the sorrel purée. Stir in the yogurt and reheat. Do not boil the soup once you have added the yogurt, as it might separate. Add a dash of pepper and sprinkle with some freshly chopped parsley before serving.

Split Pea Soup with Lovage Stock and Garlic

Lovage stock gives soup a unique celerylike flavor. Here it substitutes for the richness of a ham bone. This soup freezes well; I call it "money in the bank soup." Homemade croutons go well with it, or it is good with a heavy rye bread or whole-wheat buns. Serves 6-8.

3 cups (750 mL) dried green split peas

4 cups (1 L) lovage stock (recipe page 4)

4 cups (1 L) chicken stock

2 bay leaves

1 large onion, finely chopped

5 cloves garlic, peeled and minced

2 Tbsp. (30 mL) olive oil

dash of soya sauce

freshly ground pepper

chopped parsley or green onions, as garnish

Put peas, stock and bay leaves into a large saucepan and simmer for an hour and a half, until peas are soft and well cooked.

Gently sauté the onion and garlic in the olive oil for five minutes until soft, but not brown. Add onion and garlic to the soup mixture.

Purée the soup in a food processor until smooth. Thin with water if it is too thick. Add a dash of soya sauce and pepper to taste and heat through before serving. Sprinkle with chopped parsley or chopped green onions.

Black Bean Soup with Cilantro

Either canned or dried black beans may be used in this soup, which goes well with cornbread or muffins. Cilantro, also known as coriander and Chinese parsley, has a musky, mysterious flavor that brightens up bean recipes. It is used in Indian, Chinese and Mexican cuisines and enjoys great popularity in California. As it is available fresh in many supermarkets all winter, I include it in winter recipes. Serves 6-8.

2 cups (500 mL) dried black beans, soaked overnight

10 cups (2.5 L) chicken or vegetable broth

2 large onions, finely chopped

4 cloves garlic, peeled and minced

3 Tbsp. (45 mL) olive oil

freshly ground pepper

1 bay leaf

dash of salt

1 large bunch fresh cilantro, finely chopped

dash of hot pepper sauce

sour cream (optional)

Place the drained soaked beans in a large saucepan with water and bring to a boil. Reduce to a simmer, cover and cook for about two hours or until tender. The time will vary depending on the beans, the pot, the stove, the water and the cook. Drain water from the beans when cooked, add the chicken or vegetable broth to the beans, and set aside.

In a frying pan, sauté the onion and garlic in the olive oil until soft (about 4-5 minutes). Add to the beans and stock. Add pepper, bay leaf and salt to taste. Stir in 4 Tbsp. (60 mL) of the chopped cilantro. Simmer the soup for 30 minutes to combine the flavors.

Scoop out one cup (250 mL) of the beans and set aside. Purée the rest of the soup in batches in a food processor. To serve, reheat the soup and stir in the reserved whole beans, which will add texture to the purée. Add a dash of hot pepper sauce. Serve in warm bowls and sprinkle each bowl with chopped cilantro. Pass a bowl of sour cream on the side, if desired.

Parsnip and Potato Soup with Bay and Parsley

Parsnip has a sweet earthy flavor which makes it a favorite winter vegetable. I had a wonderful parsnip soup in a restaurant on the Mendocino coast in California. The waitress said the ingredients were simply parsnips, chicken stock and cream. Here is my version of the soup. Served with whole-wheat rolls, it makes an excellent lunch. Serves 4-6.

8 medium to large parsnips, peeled and cut in rounds

4 medium potatoes, peeled and thinly sliced

2 medium onions, peeled and finely chopped

4 cups (1 L) chicken stock

2 bay leaves

2 cups (500 mL) light cream

freshly ground pepper

dash of salt

1/2 cup (125 mL) chopped parsley

Put parsnips, potatoes, onions, chicken stock and bay leaves in a large saucepan. Bring to a boil and simmer for 30 minutes, or until all the vegetables are tender.

Remove bay leaves and purée vegetables in a food processor. Return to the soup pot and whisk in the cream. Add some pepper and salt, if desired. Heat through and sprinkle with chopped parsley before serving.

CHAPTER SIX

Winter Vegetables with Herbs

*V*egetables were a recurring theme in my childhood, starting with the first lettuce and radishes from the cold frame in early spring. They were treated with reverence, as in those ancient times (the '40s and '50s), no vegetables arrived from California and Mexico. Summers were spent picking and podding peas, and cutting beans for canning. One year Father rented a half-acre field and planted potatoes. We children were used as a slave gang when harvesting time came.

Here in our temperate climate, we can grow some vegetables all winter. The bounty of summer can also be frozen, canned, dried and stored, and of course supermarkets today have an amazing array of vegetables.

The winter vegetables at Ravenhill are planted in July, August and September. Potatoes, squash, garlic, elephant garlic, shallots and onions are stored in the garage and the barn. Broad beans, peas and tomatoes are frozen. In the garden are lettuces in winter cold frames, beets, carrots, parsnips, celeriac, leeks, kale, fennel, Belgium endive, arugula, purple sprouting broccoli and a mixture of Oriental greens. Barring a terrible cold snap, we dine off this selection until spring.

Parmesan Leek Gratin with Chives

This dish is quick to make and has a delicious, crunchy Parmesan topping. I often serve it with roast lamb. I have also substituted fennel for the leeks in this dish. Serves 4-6.

4-6 large leeks, thoroughly washed so all grit is removed

1/4 cup (50 mL) frozen chives or green onion tops finely chopped

freshly ground pepper

1 cup (250 mL) freshly grated Parmesan cheese, or use a sharp
  Cheddar or asiago

Cut washed leeks in rounds, including some of the tender green part as well. Place in a saucepan with l cup (250 mL) water. Bring to a boil and cook about five minutes until tender. Drain well.

Butter a flattish ovenproof casserole and place the drained leeks in the dish. Sprinkle the chives or green onions on top and add the pepper. Spread the grated Parmesan evenly on top of the leeks. Pre-heat oven to broil. Just before serving slide the leeks under the broiler and broil until the cheese is bubbling, crusty and golden.

Endive Wrapped in Ham with Béchamel Sauce and Parmesan

A dual-purpose vegetable, endive is good raw in salads or cooked. Its crisp texture and slightly bitter flavor contrast well with mild smooth sauces such as béchamel. I flavor the béchamel with a shallot, bay leaves and some finely chopped thyme. Omit the ham and you have a delicious vegetarian dish. Served with a green salad and a crusty loaf of bread, this is a special Sunday lunch. Serves 6.

6 endives, washed

6 slices ham, thinly sliced

4 Tbsp. (60 mL) butter or margarine

2 bay leaves

1 shallot, finely chopped

1 Tbsp. (15 mL) finely chopped thyme

1/4 cup (50 mL) flour

2 cups (500 mL) milk

freshly ground pepper

1 cup (250 mL) freshly grated Parmesan or Cheddar cheese

In a large saucepan cook the endives for five minutes in a small amount of water. Drain well. Butter a large, ovenproof baking dish. Wrap each endive with a slice of ham and place in the casserole seam side down. Set aside.

To make the béchamel sauce, melt the butter or margarine in a saucepan. Add the bay leaves, shallot and thyme. Stir well. Slowly whisk the flour into the melted butter and herbs. Keep stirring until the butter has absorbed the flour. Cook and whisk a few more minutes.

Remove from heat and slowly add the milk, whisking all the while. (I have made this sauce with skim milk and it is delicious.) Return to medium heat, add pepper and stir and cook until the sauce thickens. It will take about 5 minutes. If the sauce is too thick, add some more milk.

Remove the bay leaves and pour the sauce over the ham and endives. Sprinkle the cheese on top. Bake in a 350°F (180°C) oven for 30-40 minutes, until the top is golden and the sauce is bubbling.

Puréed Broad Beans with Italian Parsley and Garlic

Broad beans, or fava beans, are much loved by the English and the Italians; my English father grew them faithfully each year. I always freeze some broad beans for winter dishes and soups. If picked when very small, the outer skin is tender and delicious. If the skin has become tough, remove it. This dish is delicious with a small barbecued steak or lamb chop. Serves 4.

4 cups (1 L) frozen or fresh broad beans

4 cloves garlic, peeled

1 bay leaf

1 sprig winter savory

4 Tbsp. (60 mL) olive oil

freshly ground pepper

3 Tbsp. (45 mL) chopped Italian parsley

Put beans, garlic, bay leaf and winter savory in a saucepan, with water to cover. Bring to a boil and simmer for 30 minutes. Drain and remove the outer skins if necessary. Remove the bay leaf and the savory sprig.

Purée the beans and garlic in a food processor. Add the olive oil and pepper and process briefly. Serve warm, sprinkled with parsley.

Noël's Baked Beans with Herbs

Saturday night winter dinners in my childhood were baked beans, brown bread, and cabbage and apple salad. Over the years my baked bean recipe has evolved, so that now I use herbs for flavoring instead of ham or pork. Try varying the beans, mixing navy, kidney and black beans together for a bean medley. Serves 6.

3 cups (750 mL) white navy beans or black or kidney beans
   soaked overnight, rinsed and drained

2 medium onions, coarsely chopped

3 cloves garlic, peeled and chopped

a dash of rum or sherry

2 bay leaves

4 sprigs thyme

2 sprigs winter savory

freshly ground pepper

6 sun-dried tomato pieces, coarsely chopped

9 cups (2.25 L) water

1/4 cup (50 mL) molasses

1 cup (250 mL) catsup

1/4 cup (50 mL) brown sugar

2 tsp. (10 mL) dry mustard

dash of hot pepper sauce, if desired

Combine beans, onion, garlic, rum or sherry, bay leaves, thyme, winter savory, pepper, sun-dried tomatoes and water. Cook for 4 hours covered in a 350°F (180°C) oven or 10 hours in a slow cooker. If cooked in the oven, check the liquid and add more water if necessary.

When beans are tender, add remaining ingredients and stir well. Cook for another hour. Beans do vary, so if they are not tender, keep cooking them, being careful to not let them dry out. Leftovers freeze well.

Carrot Purée

Vegetable purées are a good contrast in texture and color to roasted meats. The glowing colors brighten up winter dinner plates and the smooth, nursery-food texture is very soothing. Traditionally, cream is added to purées, but I now use low-fat yogurt or low-fat sour cream, which gives the bland vegetables a lift. Purées are a perfect vehicle for chopped herbs, such as parsley, green onions, frozen chives and tarragon. For a special touch, sprinkle the purée with homemade breadcrumbs, dot with butter and put it under the broiler for a few minutes until the top is crisp and brown. Serves 4-6.

2 lbs. (1 kg) carrots, peeled, trimmed and cut into rounds, or 4 cups (1 L) squash, peeled and cubed

1/4 cup (50 mL) low-fat yogurt

2 Tbsp. (30 mL) brown sugar

1/4 tsp. (1 mL) ginger

1/4 tsp. (1 mL) nutmeg

1/2 cup (125 mL) chopped fresh or frozen herbs, such as chives or parsley

freshly ground pepper

butter or margarine, if desired

Put carrots or squash in a saucepan with water to cover and bring to a boil. Simmer for ten minutes, until tender. Drain. Purée in the food processor. Add the yogurt, sugar, ginger, nutmeg, chopped herbs and pepper, and process briefly.

Put purée in an ovenproof dish. If desired, dot the top with butter or margarine. Bake in a 350°F (180°C) oven for 25-30 minutes, until heated through.

Baked Sliced Potatoes with Rosemary and Garlic

This trio produces the perfect culinary ménage à trois. *The strong flavors suit winter cooking, but I confess I start to make this dish in the summer when we first harvest the new potatoes. If they are small I leave them whole. My favorite potatoes for this dish are rosy red Pontiacs. Serves 4-6.*

8 medium-sized potatoes, peeled and sliced, and set aside in
  water to cover

1/2 cup (125 mL) olive oil

10 cloves garlic, peeled and sliced in half

4 Tbsp. (60 mL) chopped fresh rosemary

freshly ground pepper

Preheat oven to 400°F (200°C). Layer the potatoes in overlapping rows in an ovenproof baking dish. Brush each row with some of the olive oil. Tuck the halved garlic cloves under the potatoes. Sprinkle with the chopped rosemary and pepper. Drizzle the potatoes evenly with remaining olive oil.

Cover the dish with a lid or foil and bake for 40 minutes, until potatoes are tender. Remove cover and cook another 15 minutes. Flick on the broiler to give the potatoes a last crisping just before serving.

Berlin Wall Red Cabbage

I was making a red cabbage dish for a November cooking class when the Berlin Wall came crashing down, and that is how this recipe got its name. Nearly every European country has a red cabbage recipe. It is perfect winter food, rich in color and taste, and it goes well with meat dishes and keeps well in the refrigerator. It can be used cold, as a condiment, or reheated. Serves 8.

4 lbs. (2 kg) red cabbage, finely shredded

2 cups (500 mL) beef stock

4 Tbsp. (60 mL) butter or margarine

4 Tbsp. (60 mL) cider or fruit vinegar

3 Tbsp. (45 mL) brown sugar

2 tart apples, such Granny Smith, peeled and grated

4 cloves

1 cinnamon stick

rind of one orange, grated

freshly ground pepper

1/2 cup (125 mL) red wine

3 Tbsp. (45 mL) red currant jelly

Place shredded cabbage in a saucepan. Heat stock separately and pour over the cabbage. Add butter or margarine, vinegar, sugar, apples, cloves, cinnamon, orange rind and pepper. Simmer 30-45 minutes, stirring frequently. Remove cinnamon stick. Add red wine and red currant jelly in the last ten minutes.

Mashed Potatoes and Celeriac with Parsley

While exploring new ways to prepare mashed potatoes, I came upon this combination. It was a hit at Christmas dinner — it wasn't too exotic for those family conservatives who like the same menu unchanged. It can be made a day ahead and reheated. Serves 8-10.

2 lbs. (1 kg) celeriac

8 medium potatoes, peeled and cut into quarters

1/2 cup (125 mL) milk

freshly ground pepper

1/2 cup (125 mL) finely chopped parsley

paprika

1/2 cup (125 mL) butter or margarine

Peel celeriac and cut into cubes. Place celeriac in acidulated water immediately after peeling, to stop it from discoloring. (To make acidulated water, put 3 Tbsp./45 mL lemon juice into 1 quart/1 L water.)

Cook potatoes until tender, 20-25 minutes. Drain and mash with the butter and milk. Set aside.

Cook the cubed celeriac until quite tender when pricked with a fork. Drain and purée the celeriac in a food processor until very smooth.

Stir the celeriac into the mashed potatoes and mix well with a whisk. Add pepper and chopped parsley. Place in an ovenproof casserole. Sprinkle with paprika and dot with butter or margarine. Preheat oven to 350°F (180°C) and bake for 30-40 minutes, until the mixture is heated right through.

Andrew's Baked Elephant Garlic with Balsamic Vinegar

This recipe evolved because the gardener realized one winter that the cook was not using up the supply of elephant garlic that he had carefully grown. The gardener prepared it and cooked it alongside a roast of lamb. It was very good and has become a family staple. Serves 4-6

8-12 cloves elephant garlic, peeled

3 Tbsp. (45 mL) olive oil

1/4 cup (50 mL) white wine

1/4 cup (50 mL) chicken stock

2 Tbsp. (30 mL) balsamic vinegar

Cut big garlic cloves in half. In a small, heavy frying pan on medium-high heat, cook the garlic in the oil for 5-10 minutes. Add white wine, chicken stock and balsamic vinegar. Bake covered in a 375°F (190°C) oven for 45 minutes. Check after 30 minutes and add more liquid if necessary (stock or wine). The cloves will be soft and caramelized when cooked. Serve as a side dish with a roast.

CHAPTER SEVEN

Favorite Fish and Seafood Dishes

ish and herbs are good companions, and the use of herbs reduces the need for salt. The health benefits of fish are much discussed these days when many people are reducing their intake of red meat. It is also quick to cook and versatile, and can make an elegant company dish or a speedy supper for busy working families. Markets carry a good selection of frozen and fresh fish for the cook to choose from. With air transportation, all kinds of fish are now available.

Mild-flavored fish becomes much more exciting when cooked with herbs and served with a herb-flavored sauce. Dill, tarragon, sorrel, parsley and cilantro are my favorite herbs to use with fish. The first three freeze well, and parsley and cilantro are almost always available in markets. Using your collection of frozen herbs as a source for sauces, you can improvise and brighten up any fish or seafood dinner. Also remember, there are always those two faithful standbys, lemons and parsley.

Scallops with Rosemary and Lemon

Scallops are the perfect, fresh, almost instant food, for they taste delicious, cook quickly and are not fattening. This recipe is adapted from one by Marcella Hazan whose three books, Classic Italian Cooking, More Classic Italian Cooking, *and* Marcella's Italian Kitchen *have been an ongoing correspondence course for me in Italian cooking. It is simple, robust food made with fresh ingredients from the garden or market, with lots of olive oil, garlic and herbs. Serves 4.*

1 1/2 lbs. (750 g) scallops

4 cloves garlic, peeled and thinly sliced

1/4 cup (50 mL) olive oil

2 tsp. (10 mL) finely chopped fresh rosemary or 1 tsp. (5 mL) dried

freshly ground pepper

3 Tbsp. (50 mL) fresh lemon juice

lemon slices, as garnish

rosemary sprigs or parsley, as garnish

Wash scallops and pat dry. In a large frying pan, on medium heat, cook the garlic in the oil. Stir for a few minutes, taking care not to overbrown the garlic. Add the scallops, rosemary and pepper. Turn the heat up to high for a few minutes, stirring constantly, until scallops turn white. Add lemon juice, stir and serve at once on a bed of rice with slices of lemon. Decorate with a few rosemary sprigs.

Sautéed Trout with Sorrel and Lemon

The frozen puréed sorrel in this recipe adds a tart lemon flavor to the mild trout. It is delicious served with wild or brown rice. Serves 2.

4 Tbsp. (60 mL) butter or margarine

2 trout (about 8 oz./225 g)

1/4 cup (50 mL) frozen puréed sorrel, thawed (recipe, page 3)

juice of 1/2 lemon

freshly ground pepper

4 Tbsp. (60 mL) chopped parsley

lemon slices, as garnish

Melt the butter in a frying pan. Sauté the trout about 4 minutes on each side, until lightly browned. Remove trout to a warmed platter.

Stir the puréed sorrel and the lemon juice into the pan with remaining butter. Stir well and heat through. Add a sprinkling of pepper. Pour the sauce over the trout and sprinkle with chopped parsley. Decorate with lemon slices.

Crab Cakes with Tarragon and Chives

If you have stashed away some tarragon and chives in your freezer, use them for this recipe. If not, use some fresh cilantro and green onions from the market. These cakes make a first course for a dinner party, a nice addition to a buffet brunch or a lovely lunch, with a salad. Serve with a salsa or red pepper jelly. Serves 4.

1/2 lb. (250 g) crab meat

3 Tbsp. (45 mL) chopped chives

2 Tbsp. (30 mL) chopped tarragon

1 egg, beaten

3 Tbsp. (45 mL) mayonnaise

dash of cayenne pepper

1 cup (250 mL) fresh breadcrumbs

vegetable oil

In a bowl, combine the crab meat, herbs, egg, mayonnaise, cayenne and 2 Tbsp. (30 mL) of the breadcrumbs. Mix well and form into six or eight cakes. Coat each cake with breadcrumbs, pressing the crumbs into the cakes.

In a large skillet, heat the oil on medium heat. When hot, add cakes and cook 3-5 minutes on each side, until the outside is crisp and golden. Place on paper towels to drain. Serve warm.

Tuna Cilantro Pâté

Serve this new take on the old reliable tuna sandwich, on crackers or toast, in tomatoes, or in small lettuce cups.

1 7-oz. (113-g) tin of good-quality chunk tuna

1/4 cup (50 mL) chopped fresh cilantro

3 Tbsp. (45 mL) fresh lemon juice

1/4 cup (50 mL) low-fat cottage cheese

1 Tbsp. (15 mL) capers

freshly ground pepper

sprigs of cilantro and a thin slice of lemon, as garnish

Purée all ingredients except for the garnish in a food processor. Place in a bowl and decorate with a few sprigs of cilantro and a thin slice of lemon.

Baked Salmon with Mustard Dill Sauce

These baked salmon steaks are perfect for a company dinner. Use parsley and green onions if no dill is available. Serves 4.

4 salmon steaks, about 1 inch (2.5 cm) thick

freshly ground pepper

4 Tbsp. (60 mL) chopped dill

1 cup (250 mL) dry vermouth

4 Tbsp. (60 mL) fresh lemon juice

Mustard Dill Sauce (recipe follows)

Preheat oven to 350°F (180°C). Place the four salmon steaks in a large, buttered, ovenproof dish. Sprinkle the steaks with freshly ground pepper and dill, and pour the vermouth and lemon juice over them. Cover with a lid or aluminum foil and bake for 20-30 minutes. Serve with Mustard Dill Sauce.

Mustard Dill Sauce

This yellow, lemony, dill-flecked sauce can be made ahead of time and refrigerated for up to 5 days. It goes well with all kinds of seafood, such as crab, shrimp or cold salmon.

1 egg plus 1 yolk, at room temperature

2 Tbsp. (30 mL) fresh lemon juice

2 Tbsp. (30 mL) sugar

2 Tbsp. (30 mL) Dijon mustard

1 Tbsp. (15 mL) grated lemon rind

1/2 cup (125 mL) chopped dill, fresh or frozen

1 cup (250 mL) safflower oil

Blend egg and yolk in a food processor until creamy. Add lemon juice, sugar, mustard, lemon rind and dill. Process until smooth. Add oil in a slow, thin stream, with the motor running. The mixture should thicken. Refrigerate if not used immediately.

Parsley Lemon Butter

Use this on practically any fish, including salmon, cod, red snapper and halibut. It melts on the cooked fish for an instant sauce. It tastes good on vegetables, too. Makes 1/2 cup (125 mL).

1/2 cup (125 mL) butter or margarine

2 Tbsp. (30 mL) fresh lemon juice

3 Tbsp. (45 mL) finely chopped parsley

dash of hot pepper sauce

Mash all ingredients by hand or in a food processor. Put in a pretty crock, cover with plastic wrap and refrigerate. The butter will keep a few weeks in the refrigerator or it can be frozen.

CHAPTER EIGHT

Five Winning Winter Salads

*T*here is more to a salad than lettuce. For winter salads I like the sturdy crunch of red and green cabbage, the peanutty taste of arugula, the anise flavor of fennel and the amazing colors of red and yellow peppers. Searching for new and unusual salad greens can become a passion. Trips to Chinatown or ethnic markets can turn up interesting greens such as cilantro, watercress, daikon radish and Chinese cabbage. Marinated vegetables such as peppers, carrots, and artichokes are good additions. Add citrus juices, Dijon mustard and herbs from your garden, window sill or freezer to your dressings to spark them up.

Remember, too, that the old staple winter vegetables can all be used in salads, either raw or cooked. Cabbage, carrots, onions, turnip, celeriac and potatoes all make delicious winter salads. Leftover vegetables can gain a new life with a zesty vinaigrette — use the herbal vinegars made in the fall for dressings. Here are a few recipes that will liven up your winter dinners.

Red December Salad

This red, red salad looks very dramatic on a white plate and the citrus dressing gives it a fruity, tangy taste. The addition of cilantro or parsley gives extra flavor and color contrast. Serves 4-6.

1 cup (250 mL) cooked red kidney beans (canned may be used)

1 red onion cut in fine rings

1 diced red pepper, with seeds and white fiber removed

Citrus Dressing (recipe follows)

1 medium-sized red cabbage, finely shredded

1 cup (250 mL) finely chopped parsley or cilantro

Combine drained beans, red onion and red pepper in the bottom of a large salad bowl. Add enough dressing to moisten and set aside to marinate for 30 minutes.

Mix in the shredded cabbage, add the remaining dressing and toss well. Sprinkle the top with the chopped cilantro or parsley. To serve, line a large flat dish with green romaine leaves or savoy cabbage leaves and spoon the red salad onto it.

Citrus Dressing

1/2 cup (125 mL) freshly squeezed orange juice

2 Tbsp. (30 mL) Dijon grainy mustard

1/4 cup (50 mL) olive oil

3 Tbsp. (45 mL) Japanese rice wine vinegar

1/4 cup (50 mL) honey

3 Tbsp. (45 mL) poppy seeds

2 shallots, finely chopped

1 Tbsp. (15 mL) finely grated orange rind

freshly ground pepper

Mix all the ingredients in a bottle with a tight lid and shake well.

Arugula and Pine Nut Salad

Considered a peasant green in Italy, where it grows wild, arugula has a trendy reputation in North America. Easy and quick to grow, it is a staple in our salads and the tougher leaves are delicious in soup or stir-fry. At Ravenhill Farm, the last crop of arugula is planted in September. With luck it will stand there well into the spring. We plant again in late February or March and then every few weeks until September. Spinach is a good substitute for arugula. Serves 2.

1/4 cup (50 mL) pine nuts

1 large bunch arugula leaves, washed and torn into bite-sized pieces, then spun dry in the salad spinner

4 Tbsp. (60 mL) olive oil

1 Tbsp. (15 mL) balsamic vinegar.

freshly ground pepper

Toast pine nuts on a cookie sheet in a 350°F (180°C) for 10 minutes. Set aside to cool.

Combine arugula leaves and toasted pine nuts in a salad bowl. Sprinkle the oil, vinegar and pepper on the salad and toss well.

Fennel Salad

Fennel (also called finnochio in Italian) is a cool weather vegetable that is usually available in the markets in the fall and winter. Its huge fronds grow above the bulbous vegetable; I use the leaves for a bouquet in the kitchen and snip them into everything I cook for a week. This crisp, anise-flavored, celerylike vegetable makes a very good palate-cleansing salad. Serves 4.

1 fennel bulb, washed

4 Tbsp. (60 mL) olive oil

2 tsp. (10 mL) fresh lemon juice

freshly ground pepper

chopped fennel leaves

Cut the fennel bulb vertically into quarters and then dice. Remove any brown bits. Place the diced fennel in a bowl and sprinkle with the olive oil, lemon juice, pepper and chopped fennel leaves. Toss well. This salad keeps for several days in the refrigerator.

Watercress and Red Onion Salad with Raspberry-Yogurt Vinaigrette

Watercress or landcress are often included in herb books. Land-cress can be substituted for watercress; they are peppery first cousins, with delicious, dark green leaves that can be used in soup or stir-fry, as well as salads. Watercress is usually available in Chinatown markets all year round. Serves 4.

4 cups (1 L) watercress or landcress greens

1 medium-sized red onion, finely chopped

Raspberry-Yogurt Vinaigrette (recipe follows)

Carefully wash greens, discarding the tough stalks. Spin dry in a salad spinner. Combine greens and onion in a salad bowl. When ready to serve, toss with the dressing.

Raspberry-Yogurt Vinaigrette

This low-fat dressing has a zesty fruit flavor that pairs well with watercress and onion.

1/2 cup (125 mL) low-fat yogurt

2 Tbsp. (30 mL) raspberry vinegar

1 Tbsp. (15 mL) Dijon mustard

1 Tbsp. (15 mL) mayonnaise

1 clove garlic, peeled and crushed

1 tsp. (5 mL) sugar

freshly ground pepper

Mix all the ingredients in a bowl and whisk well. Refrigerate until ready to use.

Grated Carrot Salad with Horseradish Dressing

Horseradish is a sturdy perennial herb. If you fertilize and water it well in the summer, there should be some juicy roots waiting for you in nature's own root cellar. In the fall, grub around for a root. Peel it and chop it into chunks. Put it into the food processor with enough wine vinegar to make a smooth sauce. If you have no horseradish in your garden, you can make this with a store-bought jar of horseradish. Serves 4-6.

4 large, crisp carrots, washed, peeled and grated

4 green onions or shallots, finely chopped

2 Tbsp. (30 mL) prepared horseradish

1/2 cup (125 mL) mayonnaise

dash of tamari soya sauce

Mix the carrots and onions in a salad bowl. Combine horseradish, mayonnaise and tamari sauce and mix well. Add to vegetables and toss. It will keep for a few days in the refrigerator.

CHAPTER NINE

Christmas Pleasures

hristmas is the red glow in the dark gray month of December. Long ago, when our ancestors celebrated the winter solstice, they were probably celebrating the amazing fact of their survival for another year.

I have been cooking and preparing for Christmas for thirty years and still find December an exciting time. The passing years have not jaded my enjoyment in preparations.

The preparations for Christmas in my childhood on northern Vancouver Island in the forties and fifties were both mysterious and exciting. My mother made up to two hundred mince pies. The turkey usually weighed about twenty-five pounds (eleven kilograms). One year it was so large it was cooked at the local bakery. We children polished the silver.

Mother made heavy dark fruitcakes that were studded with almonds and we were forbidden to steal the nuts off the cakes. Salted almonds for snacks were made by boiling, skinning, roasting and salting the nuts before putting them in little silver bowls. Bread sauce, the great English poultry extender, was made in a double boiler. In the center of the sauce was an onion studded with cloves. The turkey was stuffed with sage-flavored sausage meat at one end and bread, onion and sage stuffing at the other. Hard sauce for plum pudding was made with a pound of butter, drips of rum, and icing sugar. Someone had to beat and beat the mixture with a wooden spoon until it was creamy and perfect.

Unmarried teachers far from home were invited, and a bachelor lawyer with a Santa Claus tummy and laugh always came and ate huge helpings while we children stared at his stomach in amazement.

Over the years certain recipes have become favorites and I make them every year for family and friends. Celebrating Christmas is a life-affirming act in the middle of winter and to me it is the best winter pleasure of all.

The following recipes are a collection of appetizers, condiments, food gifts, and Christmas dishes that can be made and enjoyed all through December for parties and family gatherings.

Condiments for Christmas

*T*hese recipes will flavor your Christmas food and make perfect gifts. It is fun to make gift baskets of your own condiments. During the year I hunt for unusual baskets and bottles for my Christmas packages.

Onion Jam

Onion Jam has a rich intense taste that goes very well with roasted meats, quiche, chicken and cold cuts. Make it with red or yellow onions. It keeps well in the refrigerator, but it's so good that it won't last. Makes 3-4 cups (.75-1 L)

2 lbs. (1 kg) chopped red or yellow onions

4 Tbsp. (60 mL) butter or margarine

dash of salt

2/3 cup (150 mL) sugar

1/2 cup (125 mL) dry sherry

4 Tbsp. (60 mL) herb vinegar

1/4 cup (50 mL) honey

freshly ground pepper

dash of cayenne pepper

Put onions and butter or margarine in a saucepan and sauté for a few minutes. Add remaining ingredients, lower heat and simmer until the mixture has thickened, about 45 minutes. Taste for seasoning. Add more cayenne if you like it hotter. Store in the refrigerator in a sterilized jar. Warm to room temperature before serving.

Special Port Wine Jelly

Early every December I make this jelly and later give it to special friends. It is a deep ruby color and is the perfect condiment for ham, roast lamb, game or cold turkey. Makes 4 small jars (about 2 cups/500 mL).

2 cups (500 mL) port wine

3 cups (750 mL) sugar

1/4 tsp. (1 mL) powdered cinnamon

1/4 tsp. (1 mL) powdered cloves

5 whole cloves

1/2 bottle liquid pectin

Measure the wine into a saucepan. Stir in the sugar and spices and mix well. Heat and stir constantly until the sugar is dissolved. Add pectin and bring to a boil for one minute. Remove from heat and skim off the foam. Pour into sterilized jelly jars and seal with paraffin wax 1/8 inch (3 mm) thick, or use canning lids.

Red Pepper Christmas Savory Jam

In September when I have a glut of red peppers, I freeze some, and then in November and December I make this cheery red jam. It is such a hit it is often eaten before I can give it away. Serve it with bagels and cream cheese, baked ham, chicken, pâté, muffins and scones. The vinegar and sugar give it a sweet and sour flavor. Makes 2 cups (500 mL).

6-8 sweet red peppers

2 Tbsp. (30 mL) salt

1 cup (250 mL) red wine vinegar

2 cups (500 mL) sugar

a good dash of hot pepper sauce or cayenne pepper

Cut peppers in half and seed them. In the food processor, grind them coarsely. Place in a bowl, add salt and cover with plastic wrap. Leave overnight in a cool place.

The next day drain off half the liquid. Combine the ground peppers, remaining liquid, vinegar, sugar and cayenne in a saucepan. Bring to a boil and reduce to a simmer. Cook for one hour, until thickened, stirring occasionally. When thick, pour into sterilized jars and either seal with paraffin wax or refrigerate. Jam will keep for up to 3 months refrigerated.

Herbed Mustard

Use some of your frozen herb cache for this mustard; either chives or tarragon are very good. The mustard will keep well in the refrigerator for several months. Decorated with a pretty label telling which herb you have used, the jars can be included in a gift basket. Makes 2 cups (500 mL).

1 cup (250 mL) dry mustard

1 cup (250 mL) herb-flavored vinegar

1 cup (250 mL) brown sugar

4 eggs, beaten

1/2 cup (125 mL) chopped herb of choice

Mix the dry mustard and vinegar in a bowl and let soak for 4-5 hours or overnight.

Combine the mustard-vinegar mixture, sugar and eggs in a heavy-bottomed saucepan or double boiler. Cook for 15 minutes, whisking occasionally, until it is thick and smooth. Add the chopped herb and mix well. Pour into sterilized jars, cover and refrigerate.

Vinaigrette de Your House

Your own house dressing could make you famous among your friends — look what it did for Paul Newman. Never tell anyone how easy it is. Use this vinaigrette as the basis for your own personalized dressing, then vary the oils and vinegars, experiment with herbs, garlic and shallots, find a secret ingredient that gives the dressing a new taste. One friend adds a dash of maple syrup. Vinaigrettes are an ongoing experiment. Each time you can make a new creation. Makes 1 cup (250 mL).

1/4 cup (50 mL) herbed wine vinegar, rice vinegar, balsamic vinegar, or lemon or lime juice

3/4 cup (175 mL) olive or other vegetable oil

1 Tbsp. (15 mL) Dijon or other mustard

1/4 cup (50 mL) chopped herb of choice

1 tsp. (5 mL) sugar

1 clove garlic, peeled and crushed, or one shallot, finely chopped

Mix all ingredients in a bowl. Beat well with a whisk, or put all ingredients in a jar with a tight-fitting lid and shake well. Store in the refrigerator and bring to room temperature before you toss the salad.

Rhubarb Chutney

Thick, rich, tart and darkly spiced, this chutney is delicious with curry dishes and cold meats and helps make leftovers more interesting. December is a good month to do a freezer inventory. I usually find several bags of frozen chopped rhubarb and the house fills with wonderful spicy smells. Makes 1 quart (1 L).

2 cups (500 mL) cider vinegar

2 lbs. (1 kg) brown sugar

2 lbs. (1 kg) rhubarb, chopped into 1/2-inch (l-cm) pieces

1 lb. (500 g) Sultana raisins

1 large fresh ginger root, peeled and grated

5 cloves garlic, peeled and chopped

3 lemons, thinly sliced

1/2 tsp. (2.5 mL) cayenne

Place the vinegar and sugar in a heavy-bottomed saucepan and bring to a boil. Add all the other ingredients and lower the heat to simmer. Cook without a lid for two or three hours. The chutney should be thick and dark. Put in small sterilized jars and seal.

Cumberland Sauce

A traditional English sauce for game, ham or turkey, this sauce has a fruity, citrus, wake-up flavor. I serve it with roast pheasants raised by a neighbor. Makes about 1 1/2 cups (375 mL).

peel of one orange

1/2 cup (125 mL) red currant jelly

1/2 cup (125 mL) fresh orange juice

1/3 cup (75 mL) port wine

2 Tbsp. (30 mL) fresh lemon juice

1 tsp. (5 mL) dry mustard

1/2 tsp. (2 mL) powdered ginger

Thinly peel the orange (making sure not to get the pith) and place in a saucepan with water to cover. Boil for 1 minute, drain and cut peel into fine shreds. Set aside.

Mix jelly, orange juice and port in a saucepan and stir well. Add lemon juice, mustard and ginger, and mix well with a whisk. Heat and stir until the jelly melts and the sauce is smooth and liquid. Add orange peel. Serve hot. It can be made ahead and reheated just before the bird or roast is to be served.

Puréed Red Pepper with Parsley and Shallots

In wintertime, red vegetables and sauces brighten up plates and your palate. This purée can be served warm as a sauce on pasta, chicken or grilled meats. For a different color note, make it with green or yellow peppers. Keep some on hand in the refrigerator or freezer; it makes an instant sauce for many dishes. Makes about 3 cups (750 mL).

4-6 large red peppers

4 Tbsp. (60 mL) olive oil

1/2 cup (125 mL) water

freshly ground pepper

2 shallots, finely minced

a dash of balsamic vinegar

3 Tbsp. (45 mL) freshly chopped parsley

Core and seed peppers. Remove white membrane, and cut peppers in slices. Sauté in a large frying pan with the olive oil for 3-4 minutes Add the water, pepper and shallots, and gently cook with a lid on for 10 minutes, or until the peppers are soft. Remove from heat and drain.

Purée the peppers in the food processor until smooth. Add a dash of balsamic vinegar. Refrigerate or serve warm. Before serving, sprinkle purée with chopped parsley.

Herb Butters

Herb butters are so simple to make and very flavorful. They keep in the refrigerator for several weeks and in the freezer for 3-4 months. A crock of herb butter makes a charming gift, and I look for attractive small pottery crocks at fall craft fairs. The butter and herbs can be mashed by hand or mixed in the food processor. Try adding a chopped clove of garlic or a shallot for stronger flavor. Once you have made herb butter, where should you use it? Herb butters can be used for everything — pancakes, grilled steaks, hot vegetables, biscuits, toast, hot French bread, fish, omelets, and sautés. Makes about 1 cup (250 mL).

1 cup (250 mL) butter

1 cup (250 mL) washed, chopped herbs (chives, tarragon, parsley, cilantro, basil, sage, garlic, shallots, rosemary)

2 tsp. (10 mL) lemon juice

Choose one herb or vary the flavor by using a combination of herbs. Mash all the ingredients with a fork or purée in a food processor. Place in a crock, cover, and refrigerate. To freeze, put herb butter on wax paper or foil and shape into a log. Wrap well and freeze. Cut off as much as you need and return roll to the freezer.

Christmas Appetizers

*T*he two requirements for Christmas appetizers is that they taste wonderful and can be made fairly quickly. Start with good fresh ingredients and add herbs for flavor and your appetizers will be a hit with family and guests.

Noël's Smoked Salmon Herb Dip and Spread

This is made every Christmas. The dip is a pretty pale pink flecked with green. Serve it with hot French bread, crackers or bagels. The herb varies, depending on what I have on hand in the garden and in the freezer. Some Decembers there is still chervil growing in the garden or I use frozen chives, tarragon, fresh parsley and green onions. Makes 1 cup (250 mL).

8 oz. (250 g) cream cheese

1/4 cup (50 mL) skim milk cottage cheese

1 Tbsp. (15 mL) lemon juice

1/2 cup (125 mL) chopped herb

4 oz. (115 g) smoked salmon (lox-type)

freshly ground pepper

2 shallots, peeled

Combine all ingredients in a food processor. Process until smooth and well mixed. Serve in a bowl with crackers or raw vegetables on the side.

Dilled Shrimp with Rye Bread

A simple, elegant hors d'oeuvre that is appealing because it is a contrast to the rich food often served at this season. Serve it with very thinly sliced rye bread. A pot of herbed butter goes well with the shrimp. Makes 4-6 cups (1-1.5 L).

3 lbs. (1.5 kg) freshly cooked shrimp

1/4 cup (50 mL) fresh lemon juice

1 bunch finely chopped dill (use frozen, or fresh if you are lucky enough to find it)

freshly ground black pepper

2 lemons, thinly sliced

1/4 cup (50 mL) chopped parsley

Rinse shrimp under cold water in a colander. Shake the moisture off. Place shrimp in a bowl and stir in the lemon juice, chopped dill and pepper. Mix well. Place on an attractive platter and decorate with the lemons, parsley and extra dill.

Crab Dip with Cilantro and Green Onions

You can use fresh, canned or artificial crab meat for this dip. It can be served warm with French bread as well as cold with vegetables and crackers. Makes 1 cup (250 mL).

2 7-oz. (113-g) tins of good-quality crab meat or two cups (500 mL) fresh or artificial crab meat

1 shallot, finely chopped

1 clove garlic, finely chopped

2 hard-boiled eggs, finely chopped

1 Tbsp. (15 mL) Dijon mustard

1 Tbsp. (15 mL) lemon juice

1 tsp. (5 mL) horseradish

1/2 cup (125 mL) mayonnaise

1/2 cup (125 mL) low-fat yogurt

freshly ground pepper

dash of hot pepper sauce

1/2 cup (125 mL) chopped herbs (cilantro, parsley and green onions)

paprika, as garnish

parsley and cilantro, as garnish

Gently mix all ingredients together in a bowl. Add more mayonnaise or yogurt if the mixture is too thick. Put dip in a bowl, dust with paprika and sprinkle chopped parsley or cilantro over the top.

Marinated Goat Cheese

Goat cheese makes a pretty addition to a Christmas buffet table, sitting in a glass jar in oil, surrounded by herbs. This is a very old method of preserving cheese; the cheese takes on the flavor of the herbs used.

3-4 small goat cheeses

2/3 cup (150 mL) olive oil

fresh sprigs of rosemary

4 coriander seeds

4 allspice seeds

sprigs of thyme

sprigs of winter savory

sprigs of fennel

6 peppercorns

Put all ingredients in a large glass jar with a good lid. Some Provençal cookbooks suggest storing for a month in a cold place, replacing the cheeses as you use them. I have eaten the cheese after a week of marinating and it is delicious. The flavor gets stonger the longer it is marinated. Serve with bread, toast or crackers.

Avocado Cilantro Spread

The buttery flavor of the avocado contrasts well with the pungent cilantro. Buy avocados ahead of time and ripen them on the counter in a paper bag — a secret I learned when staying on an avocado farm in California. Makes 1 cup (250 mL).

2 ripe avocados, mashed

1/2 cup (125 mL) finely chopped cilantro

1 Tbsp. (15 mL) lemon juice

freshly ground pepper

1 shallot, peeled and finely minced

Mash and mix all ingredients together in a bowl. I like to serve it on hot toast fingers or melba toast.

Stilton Brandy Spread

A surfeit of Stilton cheese brought home from England had to be used up and this spread was the result. It has a piquant flavor and keeps well in the refrigerator. Makes 1 cup (250 mL).

1/2 lb. (250 g) Stilton cheese (or blue cheese)

1/4 cup (50 mL) brandy

1/4 cup (50 mL) unsalted butter

freshly ground pepper

dash of hot pepper sauce

fresh bay leaves, as garnish

Hungarian paprika, as garnish

Purée all ingredients in the food processor except the bay leaves and paprika. Place in a serving crock. Refrigerate for a few days to let the flavors develop and mellow. Before serving, decorate with bay leaves and dust with paprika.

Caviar Pie

Years ago I discovered this sensuous, glamorous appetizer in a San Francisco Junior League cookbook. This adaption has become a family favorite. Serve it at an elegant Christmas brunch or cocktail party. It always disappears. Serves 10-12.

4 hard-boiled eggs, chopped

4 Tbsp. (60 mL) soft butter

1/2 cup (125 mL) finely chopped red onion

1 can of anchovies, drained, rinsed and minced

3 Tbsp. (45 mL) mayonnaise

1/4 cup (50 mL) chopped parsley

4 oz. (115 g) caviar (black or red lumpfish caviar is fine)

juice of 1/2 lemon

1 cup (250 mL) sour cream

chopped parsley, as garnish

Combine eggs, butter and half the chopped onion, and spread on the bottom of a 9-inch (23-cm) glass or china pie plate. Refrigerate for 30 minutes.

Mix together the anchovies, mayonnaise and parsley, and spread on top of the egg mixture. Mix the caviar, the remaining chopped onion and lemon juice and spread on top of the anchovy layer. Just before serving, ice with the sour cream. Sprinkle a little extra chopped parsley on top. Serve with crackers or toast points.

Chicken Legs with Hoisin Sauce and Grated Lemon Rind

Here is a substantial dish to add to the Christmas buffet table. You can substitute chicken wings or, for dinner, chicken breasts. I often use Chinese sauces and condiments in the winter when my herb supply is low. Hoisin sauce is made of sugar, soy beans, plums, garlic and chili peppers. Combined with the lemon, it gives the chicken an intense and exotic flavor. Serves 12 as an appetizer; eight for dinner.

24 chicken legs

3/4 cup (190 mL) hoisin sauce

grated rind of two lemons

6 cloves garlic, peeled and finely minced

1/2 cup (125 mL) dry vermouth or dry sherry

chopped green onions, parsley and thinly sliced lemon, as garnish

Preheat oven to 400°F (200°C). Place chicken legs in a large baking dish. Brush both sides of the legs with the hoisin sauce. Sprinkle with lemon rind and minced garlic and pour vermouth over the chicken. Bake for 35-40 minutes, turning once or twice. Add more vermouth or water if chicken seems to be getting dry. It will be a rich reddish color when done. Serve on a bed of lettuce leaves, and sprinkle with chopped green onions, parsley and very thin slices of lemon. Serve warm or at room temperature.

The Butler's Dip

A friend who was a butler in San Francisco gave me this recipe. It is heavy on the garlic, but you can vary the amount depending on your taste for garlic. Makes 1 cup (250 mL).

8 oz. (250 g) cream cheese

1/4 cup (50 mL) sun-dried tomatoes

4 Tbsp. (60 mL) chopped green parsley

8-10 cloves garlic, peeled

freshly ground pepper

Place all the ingredients in the food processor and process until smooth. It will be a pale pink color. Serve with corn chips.

Psychological Almonds

A psychologist friend gave me this recipe based on one she clipped from a newspaper. The history and origin of recipes is fascinating. They have a life of their own and move through our culture with their own momentum.

4 cups (1 L) shelled almonds

1/4 cup (50 mL) melted butter

1/4 cup (50 mL) soya sauce

Preheat oven to 350°F (180°C). Spread almonds on a cookie sheet, pour melted butter over them and roast for 10 to 15 minutes. Do not overbrown. Pour soya sauce over them and stir well. Bake for another 10 minutes. Allow almonds to cool on paper toweling. Store in a clean jar until served.

Christmas Chicken Liver Pâté

This is a rich, fresh-tasting pâté that I have been making for twenty years. I use shallots, for I like their sweetish, garlicky flavor, but onions can be substituted. Makes 2 cups (500 mL).

1/2 lb. (250 g) chicken livers, membranes removed

1 cup (250 mL) chicken stock, or to cover

1 bay leaf

1/2 cup (125 mL) chopped shallots or onions

2 Tbsp. (25 mL) butter or margarine

2 eggs, hard-boiled

freshly ground pepper

a good dash of brandy

In a saucepan, simmer the livers in the chicken stock with the bay leaf for about 10 minutes. Drain and set aside, reserving the broth.

Sauté the shallots in the butter or margarine for 3 or 4 minutes or until the shallots are soft. Purée the liver and eggs in a food processor with a little of the chicken stock to moisten. Add the shallots and process until well mixed. Add pepper and a dash of brandy. Process briefly. Serve the pâté in a crock, with toast triangles.

Christmas Miscellany

*T*his is a collection of special Christmas Day dishes that I have collected and cooked over the years. Author Lin Yutang supposedly said that nationalism is the food you ate in childhood. Some of these are childhood Christmas dishes, but I have dared to trifle with the ingredients and spark them up with herbs, spices and citrus fruits.

Christmas Orange-Spice Muffins

Oranges, cinnamon and cloves make me think of winter and Christmas. My mother's stories of being thrilled to receive one orange in the toe of her Christmas stocking make me realize what abundance we now have. Here the orange and the spices are put into muffins, not a stocking. Makes about 15 muffins.

1 orange, cut into pieces

1/2 cup (125 mL) orange juice

1/2 cup (125 mL) sunflower seeds

1 egg

1/2 cup (125 mL) butter or margarine

1 1/2 cups (375 mL) whole-wheat flour

1 tsp. (5 mL) baking soda

l tsp. (5 mL) baking powder

2/3 cup (150 mL) brown sugar

1 tsp. (5 mL) cinnamon

1 tsp. (5 mL) cloves

Preheat oven to 400°F (200°C). Grease muffin tins. Process orange pieces and juice in the food processor until finely chopped. Add sunflower seeds, egg and butter or margarine, and process until mixed well.

Mix flour, baking soda, baking powder, sugar and spices together in a bowl. Pour orange mixture into the flour mixture and stir until just blended.

Spoon batter into greased muffin tins and bake for about 15 minutes. Cool for 5 minutes before removing from tins to a rack.

Oranges and Lemons Cranberry Sauce

The oranges and lemons add a new citrusy flavor to the traditional cranberry sauce. Makes 2 1/2 cups (625 mL).

1 orange

1 lemon

1 20-oz (340-g) package fresh or frozen cranberries

2 cups (500 mL) sugar

1/2 cup (125 mL) water

6 whole cloves

Grind the orange and lemon in the food processor until finely chopped. Place remaining ingredients in a large saucepan and add the processed fruit. Stir well and cook on medium heat for 10 minutes until berries pop.

Cool to room temperature and then refrigerate. The sauce should set and be thick. Remove cloves before serving. This sauce can be made ahead and frozen.

Bread Sauce

Bread sauce was probably invented to make one small chicken feed a lot of children. It is delicious with turkey, pheasant, goose or roast chicken. Some bread sauce addicts love to eat the clove-scented onion. Makes 4 cups (1 L).

1/2 loaf good white bread, cut into cubes

1 medium onion, studded with 10 whole cloves

generous dollop butter or margarine

freshly ground pepper

dash of salt

1 bay leaf

1 quart (1 L) milk

Place the cubed bread in the top of a double boiler. Put the clove-studded onion in the middle of the bread. Add the butter or margarine, pepper, salt, bay leaf and milk. Let the mixture cook and thicken over the boiling water for an hour. Add more milk if it seems to be too thick. Serve with the turkey and vegetables.

Rum-Apple-Cranberry Mincemeat

I found this recipe in a vegetarian newsletter. Lard is eliminated but there is a good, fruity, fermenty flavor. I adapted the recipe by substituting rum for apple juice and my own fruit vinegar for regular vinegar. Makes 20 cups (5 L).

6 cups (1.5 L) chopped, peeled Granny Smith apples

4 cups (1 L) dark brown sugar

4 cups (1 L) dark navy rum

4 cups (1 L) cranberries

3 cups (750 mL) raisins

3 cups (750 mL) currants

1/2 cup (125 mL) raspberry or blackberry vinegar

2 tsp. (10 mL) nutmeg

2 tsp. (10 mL) allspice

1 tsp. (5 mL) cloves

Mix all ingredients in a large saucepan and bring to a boil, stirring constantly. Reduce heat and simmer uncovered for one hour, or until thick. The mincemeat can be frozen or placed in sterilized jars and sealed.

Carrot Brandy Christmas Pudding

The puddings of my childhood were heavy with beef suet. This pudding is full of carrots and fruit — things that are good for you. The brandy gives it a rich flavor. To flame the pudding, heat some brandy in a silver spoon held over a candle. When the brandy ignites, pour it over the pudding and the holly. Rush to the table with the flaming pudding, singing "Bring in the Figgy Pudding." Collapse in your chair and refuse to do the dishes. That is work for those who did not cook Christmas dinner. Serves 8.

2 1/2 cups (675 mL) grated raw carrot

3 cups (750 mL) grated apple

2 cups (500 mL) white flour

1 cup (250 mL) blanched almonds, coarsely chopped

l cup (250 mL) currants

1 cup (250 mL) raisins

1 1/2 cups (375 mL) chopped pitted dates

4 tsp. (20 mL) baking powder

1 tsp. (5 mL) cloves

1 tsp. (5 mL) nutmeg

2 tsp. (10 mL) cinnamon

1/2 cup (125 mL) butter or margarine

1/2 cup (125 mL) dark brown sugar

1/2 cup (125 mL) brandy

2 tsp. (10 mL) baking soda

Prepare carrot and apple and set aside. Using 1/2 cup (125 mL) of the flour, dust the nuts and dried fruit. Set aside. Mix the rest of the flour, baking powder, cloves, nutmeg and cinnamon together in a large bowl.

In another bowl, cream the margarine and brown sugar together. Alternately add flour mixture and brandy to the margarine and sugar mixture. Add grated carrot and apple, floured fruit and nuts, and baking soda. Mix lightly with a spoon or your hands.

Fill greased pudding molds or coffee cans about 2/3 full. Cover tightly with foil and steam in a large container with a lid for 4-5 hours.

Make the pudding in November to allow the flavor to ripen by Christmas. Wrap in a clean tea towel soaked in brandy and store in a cool place. Serve warm with a custard sauce or hard sauce and decorate with a holly sprig.

Dolly's Hard Sauce

Hard sauce was always served with plum pudding in my family. It is my mother's recipe but she never made it — the job was always given to any person loitering around the kitchen on Christmas Day doing nothing. After Christmas the leftover sauce was put in the icebox on the back porch and we children would steal lumps of it and dash outside before we got caught. Makes 2 cups (500 mL).

1 cup (250 mL) softened unsalted butter

3-4 cups (.75-1 L) icing sugar

1/4 cup (50 mL) rum, or to taste

In a large bowl, mash the butter with a wooden spoon until it is very soft. Slowly beat in the sugar until the butter has absorbed as much as it can. It should be a pale cream color and firm. Drizzle in drops of rum as you beat in the sugar. The whole process should take about 30 minutes. Spoon the sauce onto a pretty plate and shape into a mound. Make decorative swirls with a knife and put a small sprig of holly on top. Refrigerate until the pudding is served.

Bay-Flavored Custard Sauce

Use this custard sauce on plum pudding, mince tarts or a rich chocolate cake. The bay flavor is unusual in a sweet dessert sauce. It adds an exotic touch to ordinary custard. Makes 2 cups (500 mL).

2 cups (500 mL) milk

2 bay leaves

4 egg yolks

3 Tbsp. (45 mL) sugar

2 Tbsp. (30 mL) flour

dash of salt

1 tsp. (5 mL) vanilla extract

Scald the milk with the bay leaves. In the top of a double boiler, mix the egg yolks, sugar, flour and salt. Slowly pour in the scalded milk, stirring with a whisk. Cook the custard mixture over boiling water until it thickens. Add vanilla. Strain the custard through a sieve and serve warm over your chosen dessert.

Special Holiday Drinks

*H*aving special drinks that are only made at Christmas time helps create traditions that enrich our holiday memories. They become extra-special drinks if you have added your own herbal flavors.

Herbal Liqueur

Herbal liqueurs made at home are an old custom in the South of France. Make this liqueur in September or October so it is mature by Christmas. Serve in small glasses and toast the good health of your guests and distant friends.

sprigs of tarragon, sage or thyme

4 tsp. (20 mL) sugar, or to taste

1 bottle of vodka or *eau de vie*

Wash and sterilize a 26-ounce (750-mL) bottle. Fill about half-full with washed sprigs of tarragon, sage or thyme. Add sugar (use more if you want a sweeter liqueur). Fill the bottle with vodka or *eau de vie*. Cap the bottle and store in a cool dark cupboard for at least two months. Strain with a fine sieve before serving.

Mulled Apple Juice and Rum

Homemade apple juice mixed with rum, cloves and cinnamon sticks and heated in my grandmother's huge copper jelly pan makes a wonderful drink for a Christmas party. The kitchen fills with steam and spicy smells, the windows fog up and everyone has a wonderful time. The rum can be omitted for a nonalcoholic drink. Makes 5 quarts (5 L).

4 quarts (4 L) apple juice

4 cups (1 L) dark navy rum

10 cinnamon sticks

20 cloves

2 lemons, thinly sliced

2 oranges, thinly sliced

Mix all ingredients in a large saucepan and heat. Leave simmering on the stove and let guests help themselves.

The Holiday Excess Herbal Cure

If the holidays have been too much for you, drink this potion based on a recipe found in an English herbal. I added the sage leaf for its health-giving properties.

1 egg

3 drops soya sauce

1 sage leaf, fresh, frozen or dried

Place all ingredients in blender and blend well. Drink slowly, then either take a long walk or a long nap. Happy New Year.

Bibliography

Belsinger, Susan and Carolyn Dille. *Cooking With Herbs*. New York: Van Nostrand Reinhold, 1984.

Boxer, Arabella and P. Back. *The Herb Book*. London: Octopus, 1980.

Bremness, Lesley. *The Complete Book of Herbs*. London: Dorling Kindersley, 1988.

Creasey, Rosalind. *Cooking From the Garden*. Vancouver/Toronto: Douglas & McIntyre, 1988.

Field, Carol. *The Italian Baker*. New York: Harper and Row, 1985.

Forbes, Leslie. *A Table In Provence*. London: Webb & Bower, Michael Joseph, 1987.

Foster, Steven. *Herbal Bounty, Gentle Art of Herb Culture*. Salt Lake City: Gibbs M. Smith, 1984.

Gilbertie, Sal. *Kitchen Herbs*. New York: Bantam, 1988.

Hampstead, Marilyn. *The Basil Book*. New York: Long Shadow Books, Pocket Books, 1984.

Hazan, Marcella. *The Classic Italian Cookbook*. New York: Ballantine, 1973.

Hazan, Marcella. *More Classic Italian Cooking*. New York: Ballantine, 1978.

Holt, Geraldine. *Recipes From a French Herb Garden*. London: Stoddart, 1989.

Howarth, Sheila. *Herbs With Everything*. London: Sphere Books, 1977.

Johnston, Mireille. *The Cuisine of the Sun*. New York: Random House, 1976.

Kowalchik, Claire and W. Hylton, Editors. *Rodale's Illustrated Encyclopedia of Herbs*. Emmaus, Pennsylvania: Rodale Press, 1987.

Nazzaro, Lorel. *Pesto Manifesto.* Chicago: Chicago Review Press, 1988.

Norman, Jill. *Salad Herbs.* New York: Bantam, 1989.

Rankin, Dorothy. *Pestos, Cooking With Herb Pastes.* Trumansburg, New York: Crossing Press, 1985.

Shepherd, Renee. *Recipes From A Kitchen Garden.* Felton, California: Shepherds Garden Publishing, 1987.

Strickland, Sue. *Planning The Organic Herb Garden.* Wellingborough: Thorsons, 1986.

Tolley, Emelie and Chris Mead. *Cooking With Herbs.* New York: Clarkson N. Potter, 1989.

Tolley, Emelie and Chris Mead. *Herbs, Gardens, Decorations and Recipes.* New York: Clarkson N. Potter, 1985.

Witty, Helen. *Fancy Pantry.* New York: Workman Publishing, 1986.

Ligon, Linda, Ed. *The Herb Companion.* 306 North Washington Avenue, Loveland, Colorado, 80537. Interweave Press (periodical).

Index